VESTED INTEREST

THE FLYNNS BOOK THREE

KAYT MILLER

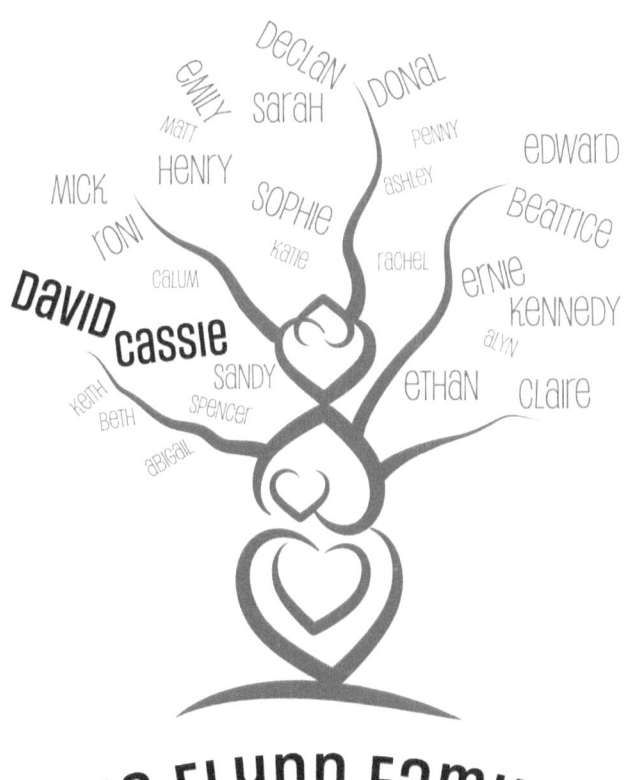

THE FLYNN FAMILY

3

VESTED INTEREST

Copyright © 2019 by Kayt Miller

All rights reserved.

No part of this book may be reproduced in any form or by any electronic or mechanical means, including information storage and retrieval systems, without written permission from the author, except for the use of brief quotations in a book review.

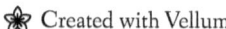 Created with Vellum

CONTENTS

1. David
2. Cassandra
3. David
4. Cassandra
5. David
6. Cassandra
7. David
8. David
9. Cassandra
10. David
11. Cassandra
12. David
13. David
14. David
15. David
16. Cassandra
17. David
18. Cassandra
19. David
20. Cassandra
21. David
22. Cassandra
23. Cassandra
24. David
25. Cassandra
26. David
27. Cassandra
28. David
29. Cassandra
30. David
31. Cassandra

32. David
33. David
34. Cassandra
35. Cassandra
36. Epilogue: David
37. Epilogue: Cassandra
38. Appendix: Hobo Signs & Symbols
39. Appendix; Quotation Credits

    Books by Kayt Miller
    Acknowledgments
    About the Author
    Thank you!
    Sneak Peek: The Importance of Being Ernie

1

DAVID

REPLACE WHAT-IFS AND SHOULD-HAVES: WITH
FUCK-YEAHS AND NO-REGRETS.

You see that quote right up there? For as long as I can remember, it's been my mantra. Well, that one plus these: No regrets. Win at any cost. And finally, Only the strong survive. Yeah, well those philosophies have served me well in the ten years I've worked at Ingot Investment Management—or IIM for short.

I started here, right out of college, at the bottom at IIM as a business analyst. That was a coup in and of itself; at that time, the job market was in the tank. My boss, Lester Ingot, took a chance. He said he "saw something in me" and went with his gut. Lester Ingot is a guy who always goes with his gut. It's what made him rich, and in my case, his gut didn't let him down. I moved up to investment banking associate much faster than the average new business analyst. Two years later, I was an associate, and by age twenty-nine, I was promoted to director and have been in this current job for four years. But now, with my latest deal, I've got my fingers crossed that I'll finally be promoted to vice president.

Hell yeah! Fuckin' VP! It'd be a major accomplishment for me, and it's happening today. I know it. I *feel* it. Because the big guy upstairs—no, not *that* big guy; I'm talking about Lester Ingot—has decided to throw a little party to celebrate the shit ton of money I just made for him—and for myself.

From my corner office, I can see caterers setting up a bar and loading the conference table with food. Lester's cheap as hell. He's got the first penny he ever made; I'm sure of it. So when he shells out money for a bar, I know this party is a big deal. All kidding aside, this could be it—the day that Mr. Ingot finally moves me upstairs to the executive floor. My dreams would become reality. Shit, I'm so stoked. I've been waiting for this for ten fucking years.

And I could use a dream come true at this point in my life. The last few months have been a fucking nightmare. Anyone who says divorce is easy is full of shit. Of course, maybe my divorce was worse than most. My ex is the spawn of Satan who is also the greediest person I've ever met. That could be why my divorce experience has been *hell*. Pure and unadulterated hell. Thankfully, the divorce was final two weeks ago, right before the huge payoff from this investment. I can't help but smirk when I think about Jen's reaction when she hears about this bump in my bank account. She'll be pissed, and that makes me smile. The woman was relentless. She wanted it all, everything I had. My lawyer, an old college buddy, was an ace. He saw through her and played her like a violin. Squeezing my eyes shut, I rub my palms over my face. I need to clear my head of all of that negative shit brought on by Jen. Today, I'm not gonna think about that divorce drama. No, today is all about me and this promotion.

Lester's email requested that the staff gather in the conference room at 12:30 p.m. At 12:20 p.m., I stand up and adjust my tie as I move into my en suite bathroom. After checking my hair in the mirror, I wash my face and brush my teeth. I take a leak, zip up, smooth my shirt down, and shake my arms out at my side. "Fuck, I'm nervous," I say to the guy in the mirror.

"What are you nervous about?" a feminine voice says from my office.

I stick my head out, "Shit, Cassie, you startled me."

She giggles. "You're talking to yourself like a crazy person in there. Everything is going to be perfect. You're going to be patted on the back, congratulated, and hopefully, we'll be promoted." My assistant is beaming at me and holding up a tie. "This one doesn't have a coffee stain on it, David."

I look down and see a small spot on my light blue tie. I'll be damned. The woman has eyes in the back of her head.

"Besides that," she continues, holding up the replacement, "this is your lucky tie."

"True." The tie's pattern is the Flynn family tartan. It's brown and orange with a tiny bit of blue in the plaid. This tie has never let me down. I wear it whenever I need something to go my way. If I need good juju, I put this baby on. I pull off the stained tie and throw it aside. Knotting my lucky tie, I grin at Cassie. "Thanks, Cassandra."

"You're welcome. Now,"—she stands with her hands on her round hips and nods at me and my tie—"you'd better get out there." She places her hand on my back and gently pushes me out the door. "Don't drink too much. You start to ramble after your second one."

I nod, heading toward the door, but she's not finished.

"Don't eat anything with garlic in it."

I nod again.

"Watch out for mustard. I can picture you with a big blob of yellow on your white shirt." She frowns. "On second thought, don't use any condiments or eat any of those little sausages in sauce that you love so much. Don't eat anything from a toothpick."

"Yes, dear," I say with a smirk. Honestly, I give her a hard time, but I don't know what I'd do without her; I would be completely lost in more ways than I can count.

"Go get 'em, tiger," she teases.

"Grrrr." I laugh. "Thanks, Cassie." I pause at the door. "You're coming, right?" Cassie hates office parties. I've found her hiding in the corner on more than one occasion during office celebrations. If I didn't insist, she'd stay at her desk instead of joining us.

"Of course, I'll be there. I heard they're having baby quiches. Plus, there will be cake. You know I never skip cake."

She means it. She does love cake. Cassandra Darrow is, well, what is the politically correct way to describe it? Full-figured? Plus-sized? No! Curvaceous! That's a good description. She's definitely curvaceous with her wide bottom and enormous ti—um, breasts. Shit, you'd think, since I used to be married, I'd be able to describe a woman's body more eloquently, but I guess I can't. One thing I can say clearly is that Cassie is nothing like my ex-wife, Jennifer. They're complete opposites, and I'm not just talking about their different body types. Cassandra is classy. She does everything tastefully. She's graceful and articulate, and she's smart as fuck. Maybe that's not the right word. Genius. The woman is a fucking genius. So, yeah, Cassie's the complete opposite of Jennifer. Jennifer's only flashes of brilliance occur when she wants something. Then and only then is she creative, manipulative, and devious as fuck.

Don't misunderstand. Cassie is more than brains—she's a beautiful woman too. Her long, dark brown hair looks like a curtain of wavy silk. In the morning when she comes into work, her hair is down. But by midmorning, she grabs a hair doohickey and winds it up into a complicated coil and attaches it—somehow—to the back of her head at the top. She always wears classy clothes too. At the office, she wears dresses or pencil skirts with pretty blouses and heels—always heels. Even the few times I've seen her in jeans, she's wearing stilettos. It's a good look. A *very* good look.

Cassandra's pale skin is flawless and looks like china—or is that porcelain? Yeah, porcelain. She wears very little makeup. She doesn't need it. Her eyes are emerald green, and she's got thick, dark lashes. Above her full lips, Cassie has the hottest little beauty mark. I love that little spot. It looks just like Marilyn Monroe's trademark spot. I've wondered what that little mark tastes like.

Shit. She's my assistant. I can't think of her that way. Besides, she's not my type.

Cassie's been with the company as long as I have—ten years. We went through orientation together, sitting next to each other during a long-ass week of meetings and training videos. If it weren't for her and her ability to make the tedium of the process fun, I'd never have made it without falling asleep. The two of us hit it off right away, and by the end of the week, we were good friends and have been ever since. I may even go so far as to say she might even be my best friend except that spot is reserved for my sister, Sandy. Or it used to be. I may have said it already, but I'd be lost without Cassie. Even if I did say it already, it's worth saying twice.

2

CASSANDRA

IT'S AMAZING WHAT YOU CAN ACCOMPLISH IF YOU
DON'T CARE WHO GETS THE CREDIT.

Oh my goodness. I'm so nervous. This is such a huge day for us—well, for David. He made a huge bundle of money for the company by investing in a company no one had even heard of. He took a huge risk for his clients and IIM. It's great working with someone who appreciates my skills and abilities and who trusts my instincts. I got really lucky that day David and I sat down next to each other at the new employee orientation. *Lucky, lucky, lucky.*

After pushing David out of the office, I use his bathroom to check my hair and makeup. I don't usually use David's bathroom, but he won't mind if I touch up my lipstick. I wince at my reflection in the mirror. "This is as good as it is gonna get, Cassandra." Sighing, I leave the bathroom and make my way to the party.

Passing by the empty desks, I hear applause and realize I'm late. I lingered too long. I make my way into the conference room and have to excuse myself as I squeeze past people. I hate having to move through crowds; I feel uncomfortable attempting to get my big bottom through a horde. I do my best to look in and around the crowd in search of David. I finally spy him on the other side of the room talking to Lester Ingot and to Lester's wife, Trixiebelle. Yup, that's really her name. She's half Lester's age and not super bright. The thing is, Trixiebelle is sort of sweet. She's nice to David, anyway. Of course, everyone is nice to David—especially people of the female persuasion. Probably due to the fact that David Flynn is drop-dead gorgeous. He's six foot two with eyes of blue and gorgeous, wavy, dirty-blond hair. Once you get past his eyes, hair, and strong chin,(which usually has a scruffy little three-day beard on it—*be still my heart!*—you can then take in the broad shoulders and muscled physique. In a few words, David Flynn is the entire package. Heck, even his teeth are gorgeous. And while I love his straight white chompers —I'll tell you a secret—his right, top canine tooth curves just a tiny bit the wrong way and is the *pièce de résistance* to David Flynn. It gives him an air of boyishness that draws the ladies like ants to a picnic.

I'd love to say that I'm immune to his looks and charm, but that would be a lie. Even on his bad days, David Flynn has my heart. As I watch him schmoozing with the boss, I already know what he's thinking. He's thinking of the promotion, he's worrying that his tie isn't straight, and he's scanning the room, looking for me. Just then, his head turns. When we make eye contact, I see him take in a deep breath before he turns back to Lester. I know I calm David like a security blanket calms a three-year-old. We're close friends. Good friends.

Hell, we started this together, and now here we are, celebrating our accomplishment in the conference room. My first job at IIM was in the secretarial pool. Ten years ago, my job in the pool was to fill in for secretaries and assistants who were taking leave or vacations. While I didn't really enjoy moving from one boss to another, I used it as a learning experience. I honed my administrative skills while also learning about stocks and investing. It was fascinating.

When David was promoted to associate, he was allowed to choose an assistant from the pool. Fortunately, he picked me, and I've been with him ever since. I know I could have moved on by now and could be doing other things, but I hate the thought of not working with David. My thoughts are interrupted when someone taps on a glass. Goodness, I'm so nervous for David. It's time for the announcement.

I watch as Lester Ingot moves to the center of the room. "Ladies and gentlemen, we're here to congratulate David Flynn on his hard work and dedication to this firm." He grins wickedly. "And to thank him for making me a hell of a lot of money." Lester laughs, followed by everyone else in the room. Even I laugh. You know how it is. If the boss does something, you follow their lead. As the laughter quiets, he turns to David. "So, tell me—no, tell all of us—what in the world made you invest in Alte Frau Cosmetics? No one had heard of the company or their breakthrough in anti-aging skin care. Are you a prognosticator?"

Laughter breaks out again. David chuckles. Turning to the group, he begins. "It's not a particularly captivating story." He looks around the room, clearly enjoying the attention. "I was in the doctor's office waiting for my appointment..."

Wait. *What?*

"My wait was long and boring. The only thing to read was a copy of a magazine called Global Cosmetics," he pauses like a pro while the group chuckles.

Nodding in response to the laughter, David goes on. "Desperate times called for desperate measures—and since my phone was dead...." More laughter. "Anyway, I picked it up and leafed through it. When an article about some R and D...." He pauses to look around the room. "That's research and development. Anyway, the title caught my eye, so I read about a German company based in Minnesota that was developing an anti-aging product that sounded promising and unlike anything else being produced today. So, I decided to check into it." He chuckles. "And that's it."

I blink, looking at David. Then I blink again and try to make sense of his words. I know my smile has faded. It's replaced by a look of confusion and disappointment. I don't understand how he could have done this. Why would he do this? We're a *team*.

"Well, my boy, thank goodness for your boring doctor's office and your impulsivity. If you hadn't picked up that magazine, we wouldn't be standing here today." Lester looks out at the group. "Let that be a lesson to all of you. Start reading boring magazines."

The group chortles, but I can barely register what's going on around me.

3

DAVID

AANNND, ONCE AGAIN, I FUCKED UP

As I tell the story—the story of how *I* discovered the obscure little company and its great new product—I watch my colleagues as they smile, nod, and laugh in all the right places. Then my eyes land on *her,* the one person in the room who knows the truth. When I see her face change, it hits me. I've screwed up. Her expression changed from a proud smile to confusion and then to hurt. I fucked up. Royally.

I stumble over the end of my fictitious tale. "So, um, yeah. That's the story. I just went with my gut and got lucky," I shrug and attempt to adopt a humbler demeanor. I'm not really humble, though. I haven't actually felt humble for a couple of decades.

Lester slaps me on the back, "Excellent, my boy. I love the way you do business and the way you go about finding prospects." He chuckles and shakes his head. "Reading magazines most of us wouldn't be caught dead reading. Global Cosmetics...." He shakes his head again as he looks out at the group. "Enjoy the food and drinks, everybody. The bar closes in twenty minutes." He walks to the door but turns to me before he leaves the room. "David?"

"Yes, sir."

"Come on upstairs. Let's have a chat."

"Yes, sir," I say, smiling. *This is it!* I turn to look at Cassandra, but she's avoiding my gaze. I walk toward her, but she turns, rushing through the crowd, heading toward the door. "Cassandra?" She ignores me. *What the hell?* "Cassie?" I repeat, louder. Working through the crowd quickly, I catch her elbow just as she steps out of the room. "Cassandra, wait up."

She turns and smiles, but the smile doesn't reach her eyes. "Oh, hey there. Great job! Congratulations, David." Her tone isn't her normal tone. It's a little shaky and just slightly chilly.

"Thanks. Uh, listen—"

Lester's assistant interrupts. "Dave, he wants to see you *now*."

"Okay." I turn to Cassie. "We'll talk later. Okay?"

"Sure thing, Mr. Flynn."

Mr. Flynn? What the fuck? In ten years, she has never called me Mr. Flynn. I glance back at Lester's assistant. She's waiting impatiently to escort me to Lester's office. Without a word, I follow the woman to the elevator. We ride up to the executive suite of offices in silence. She gestures for me to follow her to Lester's office.

"Knock before you enter," she says then sits down at her desk. I tap on his office door and wait.

A moment later, a voice sounds from behind the door. "Come in."

Pushing the door open, I walk into the inner sanctum of IIM.

"Have a seat, David."

I perch on the leather side chair directly across the wide expanse of Lester's desk and wait. Nervous, I cross one foot over my knee; then a minute later, I cross the other foot over the opposite knee. Not sure where to place my hands, I rest them on the arms of the chair, then move them to my lap, then back to the arms of the chair. Next, I set both feet on the ground and put my hands on my lap. Finally settled, I looked over at Lester and find him studying me.

"I'm proud of you, son."

He calls me "son" when I do something good... like making him a truckload of money. He clears his throat and beams at me.

"I love the way you hunt for the newest trends, David. The quality of your research before you commit to making an investment is commendable. I wish my other directors would do the same level of research. Instead, they all seem to rely on their gut instinct. That's not the way to make *big* money, is it, son?"

"No, sir." I'm a tiny bit uncomfortable accepting this praise for the background research, because that was all Cassie. I don't tell Lester about Cassie's research though because this conversation is about me.

"It's time I move you up, David. How does the title of vice president sound to you?"

"It sounds fu—uh, amazing."

Lester chuckles at my almost slip. "It *is* fucking amazing," he agrees. "The office next door is open. You can move in tomorrow. I assume you can make that timeline work?" Lester chuckles.

I look at my watch. It's 1:30 p.m. I grin at Lester. "I think I can manage that." Even if I have to stay late, I'll get it done.

"Great. I'll have maintenance bring up your things tonight. You can get settled in tomorrow. Call human resources when you get back to your office. They'll update you on your new salary and perks." He winks. When he turns away, picking up his phone, I realize this meeting's over. Walking out of his office, past his assistant, there's a skip in my step. Alone in the elevator, I wait for the doors to close and to begin my descent before I raise my fist and yell, *"Fuck yeah!"*

4

CASSANDRA

GET UP AGAINST THE WALL, I'M ABOUT TO DO DIRTY THINGS TO YOU.

I spend some extra time in my favorite stall in the staff bathroom—the one I hide in when I get stressed or overwhelmed. Leaving the stall, I go to the mirror and stare at myself. My skin is still a little more pink than usual. The scene at the party upset me, but I do understand why David said the things he did. Lester put him on the spot in front of all those people. He said what he thought he had to say. It was the truth, after all—except it wasn't *his* truth. It wasn't David in that doctor's office; it was *me*. It was *me* who read the article, and it was *me* who did the research. After I thoroughly researched the information, I presented it to David. But it really doesn't matter. The fact is, David took the risk by investing in Alte Frau, so it really is his win. I can't fault him. I know in my heart David's a good man. He's always got my back.

I wash my hands and pat cool water on my face. I'm trying to diminish the blotchiness because I don't want David to see me like this. Taking a deep breath, I square my shoulders and sternly remind myself. "Get yourself together, Cassandra." We've still got a lot to do today. I make my way back to my desk, but David's still gone. Sorting through the tasks on my desk, I place them into order of priority. I want to get them done before 5:00 p.m. Sitting down, I check out David's appointments for the rest of the day. Nothing is on his calendar. "Good. We'll get these little things ticked off my list, and then we can go home," I whisper.

"Talking to yourself again?" my friend Mallory says. She's another admin assistant for a different director.

"Yes. I can't help it," I say with a giggle.

"Here. I brought you some cake." Setting it down on my desk, I peek over to see a huge hunk of white cake with white frosting. "I saw you leave. I noticed you didn't get any, and I know how much you love cake." She winks.

"Thank you. Yeah, you know, that room was packed. I didn't feel like fighting the crowd to get to it." I laugh.

"Uh-huh, sure." She gives me a knowing glance. "Are you sure you didn't want to get out of there because your boss is a huge tool?"

Mallory knows the system David and I have adopted. She knows I have a knack for finding great investment opportunities. After I find them, I pass the information along to David. We're a team. "He's not a tool, Mal. He was put on the spot, that's all."

Vigorously shaking her head, she snorts. "Girl, you're wearing your rose-colored glasses again. That guy only looks out for number one."

No, that's not true. "We're a team," I insist.

"And there's no 'I' in team, right?" she smirks.

"Right." I know Mallory means well, but she just doesn't have the same dynamic with her boss, Andy. She's strictly an administrative assistant. I'm more than that to David.

I hear David before I see him. Looking up from my desk, I see him smiling from ear to ear. "My office, Cassie," he says, jerking his head toward his office.

I wave at Mallory before I join David in his office, shutting the door behind me. Walking up to his desk, I stand in my usual spot.

"Sit, sit." He motions for the chair.

So, I sit. Crossing my legs, I lean forward slightly. I'm ready for his news.

"It's happening," he says excitedly. "I've been promoted to VP."

"Oh, my gosh, congratulations, David!" I practically shriek. I clap my hands like an idiot, I'm so damned happy for him—for us. This is great news for my career at IIM too.

"I couldn't have done it without you, Cassie. You know that, right?"

Uh, yeah. "Yes," I say confidently.

"We need to go out and celebrate tonight."

We do? "We do!" I say, smiling. We've never gone out together after work. I've attended business dinners with him in my capacity as his assistant, but this is different. We've never been promoted to *vice president*.

"We'll go out after we pack our stuff. They're moving it upstairs for us tonight. Is there anything pressing on my schedule this afternoon?"

"No, nothing that can't be addressed tomorrow," I practically squeak. Wow, we're moving upstairs? Tonight? "This is so exciting."

"It is! Okay, can you call the mailroom and ask them to bring up some boxes? Then we can get to work."

In less than thirty minutes, maintenance has dropped off a stack of boxes—ready to be filled. Every once in a while, the hair on the back of my neck stands up. We're being watched with interest by our colleagues. I'm sure they know what we're doing, but only one or two are brave enough to wander over to ask us. I defer to David. He casually mentions he's moving his office to another part of the building. It's better to play it close to the vest until Lester officially announces David's promotion—not just David's promotion, –*my* promotion too.

By 5:30 p.m., we're packed up. David leaves notes for maintenance about breakable items; once that's finished, we walk to the elevator together. Grinning at me, he asks, "Where should we go? Are you hungry or should we just go with drinks and appetizers?"

"Drinks and appetizers."

"Great. Let's go to Emmit's."

"Sounds perfect." Emmit's Irish Pub is an institution—at least I hear it's an institution. I've never been. I know where it is; I've walked past it since it's near the bus stop, which is perfect since I'll need the bus to get home after our celebration.

We walk in silence for a few blocks. Clearing his throat, David looks at me. "Sorry about today."

I don't need to ask what he's referring to. "That's okay." And it is.

Emmit's is packed. "Wow, it's busier than it usually is on a Thursday night," says David as he holds the door open for me. "Probably because of the live band."

By some miracle, we find an empty table in a back corner. Waving over the server, David orders a whiskey. I order a bottle of Harp. Since it's so busy, we go ahead and order chicken wings and nachos. Settling back with our drinks, I smile at David. "Are you nervous?" I ask. "Vice president, that's a huge deal."

He flashes a warm smile and nods. "I'm a little nervous. But nothing I can't handle."

David always comes across as a confident guy, –even when he doesn't feel it inside. "You'll do a great job, David."

When our drinks are delivered, David raises his glass. "Cheers. Here's to women with wrinkles. Thank God for them."

I pause for a moment then giggle. The anti-aging cream got

him this promotion. "Cheers," I say as we tap our glasses together.

The food arrives, and David digs in like he hasn't eaten in days. I suspect he didn't eat lunch today. "You're hungry," I say with a giggle.

"Starving," he says with his mouth full.

I giggle again and take a chicken wing and a couple of nacho chips and put them on my plate. I don't like to eat in front of people, especially David. It's obvious I'm a large woman; he can certainly see I overindulge from time to time, but I'm still not comfortable having him see me actually eat. I nibble on my treats but concentrate on drinking fast. David seems to be keeping up with me, so we order a second, a third, and a fourth round of drinks. Sipping on the fourth drink, I realize I'm getting pretty tipsy—no, tipsy isn't accurate. I'm getting drunk. If I actually ate some of the nachos, they would absorb some of the alcohol. He's downing whiskey as fast as I'm drinking beer. For every beer I order, he orders a fresh whiskey. I'm surprised he's still upright. He must be used to the strong stuff.

"The band is pretty good, izzn't it?" he asks, slurring his words.

I hadn't been paying attention to the band. My complete focus has been on the man next to me. Also, on the four, count 'em four, women who brazenly approached our table. A couple of them even sat down in one of the two empty chairs, making themselves quite comfortable as they hit on my dinner date—er, my companion/boss. Who does that shit? Yeah, I'm fat, but it doesn't mean I'm not on a date with this man. Women suck.

Surprisingly, he's shot each of them down. Three of the women were attractive, and one of them was downright gorgeous. The old David, the pre-Jennifer David, would have grabbed that one by the hand to whisk her out of the bar. He would have happily waved at me as he left. Divorced David is much more cautious about his conquests.

I'm musing about that as David pulls me out of my own head. "Let's dance."

"Uh, what?" I squeak.

"You heard me," he says, grabbing my hand. "Let's dance. I like this song."

It's a ballad. What is he thinking? He pulls me by the hand and drags me to the dance floor. Several other couples are swaying together. Thank God, we're not the only couple on the dance floor. David slides his palm from my waist to the center of my back just above my bottom. With his other hand, he takes my hand and places it on his chest. The next thing I know, I feel myself being pulled until we're pressed together, my body, mostly my boobs, are smushed up against him. I look up at his face and blink. Even with me in heels, he stands a head taller than me. The top of my head fits under his chin.

Feeling David's hips move to the right, I nearly combust. He's using his body and hands to lead me, and I follow. I inhale. Dang, he smells so good. I breathe in his scent, letting my eyes flutter closed. I love the smell of him. I don't know if it's body soap, cologne, or just him. All I know is it's citrusy and musky all at the same time. I'd love to run my nose up the column of his neck to get a better whiff. Heck, I'd love to lick his neck just to lick something on the man, but I resist. "You can actually dance," I say with a little too much surprise in my voice.

"My mom made us all take ballroom dance lessons."

"She did?" That's unusual, but it's very nice. I've met his mom; she's been to the office a few times to take David to lunch. She's a tiny little thing, but she's sassy. I like her.

"Yeah, she thought we should all know how to dance." He chuckles. Then I feel a vibration in his chest; I realize he's humming. He's actually carrying a tune; the man can sing too?

We move around the dance floor with ease. I'm lulled into the dance until I feel his palm move lower. His huge hand is now cupping my ass. Unconsciously, I let out a little moan. Keeping his palm in that spot, David leans down like he's going to whisper in my ear, but he doesn't. He inhales and kisses me right below my earlobe. Holy Hannah Montana, that felt good. I moan again. At that moment, I feel something hard pressing against my stomach.

"Jesus, Cassie. You smell so fucking good," he says in a husky voice.

I lean back to look into his eyes. What I know are bright blue eyes are almost completely black—dilated to the point that the blue is nearly invisible. "You smell good too." Shit, I'm drunk. He's drunk. This is a huge drunken mistake—except I hope it's not the booze talking. I hope he's finally seeing something in me. Lord knows I see something in him. Before I can say another word, David leans down again and kisses me—but not on the lips. He kisses the spot above my mouth where I have a mole. His tongue swipes the same spot. Leaning toward me again, he whispers, "That fucking beauty mark makes me crazy."

"My mole?" Ugh, I hate it. Beauty mark? Hardly. Unkind comments about that mole have been directed at me since I was a young kid. Some of the lovely monikers? Witchy-poo, Moly-Wartress, Worry Wart, and, my personal favorite, Toady—it's sooooo original.

"It's a beauty mark. Marilyn Monroe had one exactly like it in the same spot," he whispers. Then he kisses it again. I know letting him kiss me on my "beauty mark," or anywhere, is a bad idea. I should walk away. He's my boss, but I've wanted him to kiss me for so long, I can't bear the thought of stopping him. Still struggling with my conscience, I feel his lips on mine—his kiss is soft and sweet. The sweetness turns decidedly wicked as he swipes his tongue across my bottom lip. Closing my eyes, I start when I feel the sting of his bite on my lower lip. It's the most erotic thing I've ever experienced. I slide my hands into his thick, wavy hair and open my mouth to his, standing on tiptoes to reach him better. I swipe my tongue into his mouth, and I hear him groan softly.

Using both hands, David grasps my ass and pulls me closer to him. When someone yells, "Get a room," he chuckles against my lips. I'm about to laugh as well when another voice yells, "Fat ass." Hearing those words is like having a bucket of ice water thrown on me. I pull away from David and rush back to our table. Grabbing my purse, I turn to leave.

"Cass? Wait up." David moves next to me. "Where're you going?"

"Home. Thanks for the beer and, uh, everything."

"Come on, don't go," he whines. I can't believe he's whining. For me.

"I, uh, it's late." I can't think of anything else to say, so I make a mad dash toward the door.

"Let me walk you out." He tosses several twenties on the table and places his palm on my back to guide me out. Outside, he guides me to the right, toward our office building.

"The bus stop is that way," I say, pointing the opposite direction.

"Yeah, and my car is this way," he says, pulling me by the hand. I don't argue with him; I follow him wordlessly. That is until he tugs me by the hand into an alley next to Emmet's. It's dark. "What...?" I start, but my next words are lost in his mouth as he kisses me. David moves closer while gently pushing me against the brick wall. Jesus, the man can kiss.

His mouth leaves mine as he places small kisses first to my mole and then down the side of my neck. He's saying something, but I can barely concentrate. He's whispering things that sound like questions. I hear, "What are you trying to do to me, honey?" His breath is hot on my neck. I raise my arms and wrap them around his neck, pulling him closer. I feel my nipples harden the second he pulls my arms above my head and, with his left hand, holds them in place. "David."

"I've got you, baby." His free hand slides over my breast. "Jesus, you're so soft, Cassie."

My nipple peaks as he uses his fingers to sweep across it repeatedly. It's been so long since anyone has touched me. The sensation is over the top good. "Oh, God," I moan.

"You like that? Do you like my hands on you, Cassie?"

"Uh-huh... yes." I gulp, trying to breathe.

Still holding my hands, he moves his free hand down my thigh to my knee. Not stopping his movements, he slides his big, warm palm up my thigh beneath my skirt, slowing slightly the closer he gets to my panties. "Are you wet for me, sweetheart?"

I nod, but I can't speak—I can only feel, especially when his finger runs back and forth over my mound. Slowly, his finger slips beneath the elastic of my panties. It dips inside, and when he groans, I feel myself get even wetter.

"Jesus, you're drenched." His breathing picks up, and so does the urgency in his hand. He releases one of my hands and brings it down to the front of his pants. Pressing my hand flat over him, I gasp. He's hard, so hard. He guides my hand, sliding first up then back down over his fly. He's big and long and rigid, and *I* did that to him. Me! Big girl, Cassandra Darrow has just turned on the sexiest man on the planet.

My internal monologue is interrupted when he grunts and unzips his pants. Pulling himself out, he takes my hand and places it on his hard length. "Keep doing that. Squeeze it." I use my thumb and fingers to grip him. Keeping my hold, I slide my hand up and down. "Faster," he groans. I move faster. My mind is divided between wanting to give him pleasure and searching for my own release. David's fingers are on my clit now, circling and sliding around, increasing the tempo to match the speed of my movements on his cock. Our breaths become pants. I'm sure we're loud enough that someone passing by the alley would hear us, but I don't care. No way am I stopping to think about anything but this. Him. God, I'm so close—about to come at the hands of my dream man for the first time ever. That is until I feel his body stiffen and hear him release a moan so loud he could be heard in Winnetka.

Stepping back, David chuckles. "Goddamn, that was hot as fuck, Cass." He pulls his hand out of my panties, and I whimper. I didn't come. I was close. So close. He wipes his hand on his pants as I look down at mine. His ejaculate is in my palm and up my arm. I reach back and find the wall and wipe my hand off there. I think I got most of it. Adjusting my skirt, I wipe my hand on that as well. Leaning down, he kisses my mole lightly then does the same to my forehead. "I'm not sure we should have done that, but I couldn't help myself." He stops for a second, like he's considering how to put this into perspective. Looking over at me, he grins. "We're celebrating!"

"Um, yeah, sure. Celebrating." I slide my palms down the front of my skirt, ensuring it's pulled all the way down. Clearing my throat, I look around for my purse. It's on the ground a foot or so from my feet; I bend over and pick it up. David runs his hands through his hair and pushes his hands into his pockets. He looks at me shyly.

"We should grab a taxi. I'm still drunk."

"Of course. Let's see if we can get one."

We leave the alley and turn right. Down the street, there's a hotel with a taxi stand in front with a line of available cabs. David opens the door of a taxi for me. I slide in far enough for him to move in, but he stands and peers down into the cab. "I, uh... well, we're going in opposite directions, so I'll grab another cab. Tomorrow, we can meet at our old office and go upstairs together. Sound good?"

"Sure. Sounds good. See you, but—" He shuts the door, cutting off my words. We could have shared a cab; I don't live on the south side anymore. I guess he forgot.

5

DAVID

YOU'RE A BAD IDEA, BUT I LIKE BAD IDEAS.

Generally, I don't mind a bad idea now and then. This time, though, the bad idea is a *really* bad idea because Cassie's my assistant—a woman I work with two hundred and sixty days a year. I'll chalk it up to the whiskey. I also can't rule out the fact that it's been eight months since I got laid—not that I got laid tonight, but Cassie's hand job was pretty spectacular. Either way, it was a fucking terrible idea. "Fuck!" I say aloud. The taxi driver hits the brakes so fast I almost brain myself on the plexiglass partition. I shake my head and wave my hand at him. "Sorry, man. I was talking to myself."

"Crazy Americans," the guy mutters.

When the taxi pulls up to my building, I toss a few bills over the seat. "Keep the change." I'm sure he does think I'm crazy, but I'd bet he's heard *and seen* worse in the back seat of his taxi. He's right, though—Americans *are* crazy.

I wave at the guy at the security desk of my building and hustle to catch the elevator before the doors close. I press the button for my floor and move to the back. It's then I see I'm not alone. I smell her before I see her; turning my head, I see a stunning blonde in a tiny cocktail dress. Without thinking, I flash my sexy smirk. I can't help it, it's almost involuntary for me. She smiles back coyly and attempts to look shy, but it's obvious this woman ain't shy.

I raise my hand to shake hers. "Hello, I'm David."

She places her fingertips into my palm and gives me that weak handshake that I hate. My dad always told us that a limp handshake says the person a) can't be trusted or b) doesn't know how to work hard. My experience has been that his observation is right on the mark. I'll give this woman a pass, though. Maybe she's a southern belle—brought up to be genteel.

In a husky voice that sounds like it's made for sin, she replies, "Dominique. It's nice to meet you."

"The pleasure is all mine." We're still holding hands when the elevator opens. She looks out into the hall and then back at me. She doesn't release my hand, and I don't release hers. "Going up?" I ask, smirking again.

She smirks back. "I thought I'd go down." She looks pointedly at my crotch.

I chuckle because, fuck, that was an awesome line. I think I love her. Yeah, *this* is my type of woman. She's tall and slim with legs that go on for miles. Her hair is a little too blonde, but it falls down her back in thick waves. Dressed for a night out, she's got on too much makeup, and there's no beauty mark above her lip. Also, her cherry-red lips aren't plump and full, but no matter. Those lips will look good wrapped around my cock.

Dominique's dress is red—what there is of it. Case in point, it's so short, if she leaned over in front of me, I'd be able to see her pussy. The front of her dress is so low, her tits are pressing out of the deep V-neck. I can almost see a nipple. Perusing her tits, I note they are smallish but nice enough. They are certainly not G's like Cassie's beautiful tits. Refocusing on this woman's chest, I watch as her nipples harden. I shake thoughts of Cassandra out of my head. This is the type of woman I need—

one who'll look good on my arm. This type of woman will represent me in the best light. I wrap my arm around her tiny waist and pull her closer; she comes willingly. "Are you sure?" I don't force a woman to suck my cock. Ever.

"Oh yeah," she says with a knowing smile.

When we reach my floor, I pull her out of the elevator by the hand. Opening the door of my apartment, I guide her with my palm on her bare lower back. Her skin is cold, and I can see her vertebrae running down her back. She doesn't have any meat on her bones, but she's still an attractive woman. "Give me a moment." I point to the bar cart over by the window. "Help yourself to a drink."

I walk into my bedroom. I need to clean up after the tryst in the alley. Stripping down, I turn on the shower and step in. Lathering up, I wash myself thoroughly as my mind wanders back to earlier in the alley. Thinking about it makes me hard again. Fuck, Cassie was hot. She can kiss too. I shut off the water and step out, grabbing my towel. Drying myself, I look into the mirror and nearly jump out of my skin when I see Dominque's reflection. She's sipping amber liquid. My whiskey. My dick is still hard from thinking about Cassie. The blonde saunters over, touching the tip of my cock.

"Nice place you've got here, Dave. What do you do for a living?" She's leaning on the counter. All of a sudden, my dick loses some of its mojo.

"Investments."

"You must be good at it." She sips her drink again.

"I do okay. What about you? What do you do?"

"Oh, a little of this and a little of that." She shrugs.

In a flash, I see the mistake looming in my near future. Jennifer and I had an exchange exactly like this the night we met. At the time, I thought her comment "a little of this and a little of that" was adorable. But what I didn't realize at the time was that she really did *nothing*. What Jen wanted was someone to fund her lifestyle, so she could continue doing *nothing*. Actually, Jennifer seemed to think that going shopping, getting massages, and having your hair and nails done was a profession for which she was well-educated. In fact, Jennifer had a fucking PhD in that shit.

I wrap the towel around my hips, hiding my now flaccid cock. "You know what? It's been a long day, and I'm beat. I don't think this is a good idea after all."

"Oh, that's a shame. You and I could have had a lot of fun." She pouts like a petulant child.

I ignore it. "Rain check?"

"Of course. I live in 333. I'm sure we'll meet again." She leans up and kisses my lips as she rubs her palm against my dick, which is, luckily, tucked safely under the towel. I don't think this particular woman's touch is going to bring him back to life tonight. Maybe not ever. Watching her leave the bathroom, I wonder about what she said. She lives in the building? I've never seen her before; maybe she's new. Then I realize I don't fucking care. I think I dodged a bullet. One of David's Rules To Live By: *Never* fuck someone who lives in the same building. Another of David's Rules To Live By: Never get your assistant off in a dirty alley. Shit. It's too late to worry about the second one. Wait…. I pause and review the scene in the alley. Shit, *did* she get off? Surely, I didn't leave her high and dry? Oh, holy Jesus. *I did*. I left her fucking hanging. And now I've got to face her tomorrow. Fuck! I'm such an asshole.

6

CASSANDRA

WHO DO YOU TURN TO WHEN THE ONLY PERSON IN THE WORLD THAT CAN STOP YOU FROM CRYING IS EXACTLY THE ONE MAKING YOU CRY?

Sliding into the taxi, I tell the driver my address. When I first moved to Chicago, I rarely took cabs—they were too expensive. On top of the expense, I was sure I would die at the hands of an erratically driving, murderous cabbie. I got over that; now, I don't even pay attention to the near-death experiences around me. *Meh, whatever.*

I close my eyes and lay my head back on the seat. David and our little tryst is on my mind. Was our little groping session in the alley a mistake? Ugh. I just made out with and fondled my boss in a dirty alley. Who was that girl back there? My thoughts turn away from the alley to work tomorrow. I feel a flash of embarrassment. What is David going to say in the morning? Wait. I *know* what he'll say. I've worked with the man long enough to know he'll say he cares about me, but it was a mistake. He'll say he's just getting over a divorce and he's not ready for anything more. He's sorry if he hurt me and I deserve better than to be fingerfucked in an alley. After that, he'll say I'm the best assistant he's ever had (I'm the *only* one he's ever had). He'll say we make a great team and he doesn't want to risk damaging our working relationship by starting a personal relationship.

"Yeah, that's what he'll say." And I'll respond with a nod, muttering mechanically, "You're right, David." And that, as they say, will be that.

I must have dozed off. I wake up to hear a thickly accented yell. "Here! You are here!"

I look up and see that I am, in fact, *here*. I pay the man and step out of the taxi. Unlocking my front door, I take three steps up into my living room and beeline it to my bedroom where I strip out of my clothes. In the bathroom, I run myself a hot bath and step into the blissfully warm water. Squeezing my eyes shut, I shake my head in an attempt to clear it. "I can't think about it anymore. Nothing's going to come from it; I know it, and he knows it. At least I got a little action," I tell myself all of that, but I don't really mean it. It's been a long, long time since I've had sex, and I can't deny that it felt so good to feel someone's hand on me—someone's hand other than mine, anyway. It's too bad he didn't help me climax, but he was pretty excited. Maybe it's been a while for him too. Poor David. I'm sure he needed it more than I did.

THE MORNING LIGHT streaming in my window is painful. Everything hurts. My head, my eyes, my eyelashes, my ears, my nose, and even my mouth—they all hurt like a mofo. My mouth is the worst; did a squirrel crawl in there and die last night? "Water," I croak to the empty room. "I need water."

I roll my big bottom out of bed and stumble into the kitchen to make a full pot of coffee instead of the half pot that I usually make. I think I'm gonna need ten cups of coffee today. At the sink, I quickly gulp down a glass of water. Once I've got a hot cup of the nectar of the gods, I step into my bedroom, walking straight to my closet in search of comfy clothes. With this hangover, I need a comfortable outfit today. I usually wear dresses or skirts, but today I'm going to wear leggings and a tunic. No worries. I'll still look professional. I'll wear a dressy tunic just like a lot of the assistants at IIM. I'll dress it up with heels and accessories.

I'm running late, so I take a quick shower, leaving my hair out of it. My hair ritual is time-consuming. So, I put it up into a messy bun—something I never do. We'll be unpacking boxes and setting up our work spaces today, so going to work dressed casually is fine. I fill a travel mug and a thermos full of coffee, adding cream and a touch of cinnamon to both containers. With my purse and coffee in hand, I'm out the door with three minutes to spare.

Unable to handle the crazies on the bus this morning, I treat myself to a taxi. At the office, I wave my security badge over the sensor, nod to the guard as I pass the desk, and hit the Up button at the elevator. I sip my coffee as I ride up and tap my foot on the ground. I'm so nervous. Part of me hopes David calls in sick today. I don't want to hear what I know I'm going to hear. Another part of me hopes... *really* hopes I'm wrong about what he'll say. On the eleventh floor, I squeeze my way through a crowd and head to my desk. My box filled with personal items still sits on top of my desk. I scan the area around my desk then into David's office. His boxes are gone, as are the boxes full of our files. "Hmm, they must not be done."

"Who's not done?" I hear his deep voice, and I turn to see a perfectly dressed and coifed David Flynn. His suit today is crisp and classic. Not only that, he's got on his lucky tie again.

I smile at him, doing my level best to pretend we didn't do dirty things in an alley together last night. *Good luck with that one, Cass.* I clear my throat. "They must not be finished taking our things upstairs. They left mine here."

"That sucks. I'll help you carry it up. But can we talk first?"

Here we go. "Sure." I step into his office, and he shuts the door behind us.

"Cassandra? About last night...."

"Yes?" I tilt my head slightly to the left to let him know I'm listening.

"Cassandra, you know I care about you, right?"

"Uh-huh."

"Because I do. It's just... I'm getting over that nasty divorce, and I'm just... I'm not ready for anything serious right now. I'm sorry."

I nod and wait for the rest. So far, I'm batting a thousand.

"I'm sorry if it hurts you, but you deserve better than me. I'm not good enough for you."

Ooh, good one. I didn't think about him saying that.

"You deserved better than being groped outside of Emmit's, for God's sake."

"I suppose—" I start to say, but he doesn't let me finish.

"You're the best assistant I've ever had, Cassandra. We make such a great team, I'd hate to fuck that up."

"You're right, David. You're absolutely right. I couldn't have said it better. Now, we'd better get up there before Lester thinks you skipped out." I laugh. I'm faking this jovial crap. It must be working because he looks so dang relieved.

"Wow, you took that really well. I thought...."

"You thought I was going to fall madly in love with you because we got drunk and hooked up?" I laugh again. Fake. "I'm a thirty-year-old woman. I know the rules of the game."

"Game? I wasn't trying to play you, Cassandra," he says, a little defensively.

"Oh, I know. You misunderstood." I place my hand on his forearm—his thick, muscled forearm. "All I meant was that you and I are fine. We're on the same page. Now, let's grab my stuff and head upstairs."

"Uh, okay." He sounds a little dazed. He smiles weakly and grabs the box of my personal stuff while I pick up the box of office supplies. We'll each have a computer and printer upstairs. I cleaned our files off our computers, but I can always ask to have my computer brought up later today. We walk side by side to the elevator as people shout out "congratulations" and "good job, Dave." The congratulations follow us all the way to the elevator. Once inside, I reach over and hit the button for the forty-eighth floor. I've only been on that floor a handful of times, so moving up to the same floor as IIM's bigwigs is a little nerve-racking. I look over and smile. David looks a little nervous too.

When the doors open, I step out first, and David follows close behind me. I stop to let him lead since I'm not sure where his new office will be. Walking down the main corridor, we turn left, pass two small offices, and stop at the third. "Here it is." David beams.

I look around the small area outside of his office. My desk is here, and David's office is beyond. Leaving my box on my desk, I gasp when I step into his office. "David, it's huge."

"That's what she said," he mutters under his breath.

I giggle, but mostly due to nervousness. It *was* funny, but it was also inappropriate. After last night, though, inappropriate seems to be our modus operandi. Shoot, I think I'm going to be nervous for a while. David sets my box of personal items on top of a coffee table that sits in front of a black leather sofa that must be seven feet long. The matching leather side chair sits next to the couch, and a tall lamp stands between the two. This office is twice the size of David's office downstairs. I look beyond his mammoth desk to the jewel of the room, the floor-to-ceiling windows. They span an entire wall, and his view of the city is spectacular. I walk to the window and look down. "You won't get any work done with this view." I smile up at him. He's not looking at me—he's busy checking out the bar. He's actually got a fully stocked bar in his office, just like on the show *Mad Men*.

Peeking around the corner, I stare into the bathroom—what a showstopper. The large steam shower is tiled in marble, and the glass vessel sink is surrounded by matching marble. I appreciate the beauty of the fixtures, but those will need to be cleaned daily. I walk back out into the office and put my hands on my hips. "This is amazing, David. You should be very proud; nobody deserves this more than you."

"Thanks, Cassie." He smiles at me warmly.

His smile makes me hope we're past what happened last night. He's about to say something when Lester steps in and booms, "Well, what do you think, my boy?"

"It's amazing, Mr. Ingot."

"Call me Lester. Please." Lester looks at me. He blinks like he's trying to place me. After a minute, something flashes across Lester's face. Looking back at David, he points to my desk. "Uh, did you meet Gretchen?"

I watch as Lester turns and walks out of the big office. I guess he's expecting us to follow. David's eyebrows lift as he gestures for me to go first. When I get to the outer office, I see Lester standing next to my desk. Looking to my right, I see a woman sitting at my new desk—a woman I've never seen before. She's so pretty, she looks like she belongs on the cover of Vogue. When she stands up, I have to look up to see her face, and I'm wearing three-inch heels. This woman has to be close to six feet tall.

She smiles warmly at David. Turning to me, her eyes squint and her nose wrinkles like she just smelled something nasty. Turning back to David, she smiles at him again just as Lester speaks. "David, meet Gretchen, your new assistant." Lester smiles at David then at Gretchen like he's just given David a shiny Christmas gift.

"My *new* assistant?" David asks, sounding confused.

He's not the only one who's confused.

"Working at this level, you need someone who really knows what they're doing."

I look at David, then at Lester, and back to Gretchen. She looks like the cat that ate the canary. "No offense, honey." She smiles smugly.

I look at David and wait for him to speak. It seems like the silence goes on forever. I can feel heat moving from my chest into my face. Sweat has begun to gather at my hairline. What the heck is he waiting for? When he finally speaks, he holds out his hand to her. "Nice to meet you, Gretchen."

I'm thunderstruck. That's all he's going to say? No, that's not it. I'm sure he's about to explain the situation to Lester and to Gretchen.

Gretchen looks at me and coos, "You're going back to the pool I'm afraid."

"To the pool?" I haven't been in the pool for eight years. Going back to the pool is a huge demotion. But this isn't going to happen. I'm not worried. David will straighten this out. He needs me. *We're a team.*

"My dear?" Lester looks at me. "They're expecting you downstairs. Report to Janice when you get there. She's got plenty of work for you to do."

Is that supposed to make me feel better? I turn and stare at David. I'm waiting for him to say *something. Anything.* But he stays mum. Seriously?

Turning away from him, I move into his office to pick up the box filled with my personal items that he left on the coffee table. I'm honestly in shock as I step back out into the outer office. Since I don't know what to say, I say nothing as I walk down the hall toward the elevator. Pressing the Down button, I can't help thinking the word "down" has many subtexts, especially right now. Everything is going down. My career, my paycheck, my self-esteem, and my affection for David. *Down. Down. Down.* I turn my head to peer back toward his office, hoping, waiting for David to come to his senses. It takes a long time for the elevator to arrive, but not long enough for David to realize that he's made a huge mistake.

Stepping onto the elevator, I turn to face the corridor. Holding my breath, I'm still holding out a last bit of hope that he'll run to me. When the elevator doors slide shut, I lose it. I sob all the way to the first floor. The second the elevator stops on one, I decide I'm done crying. So, when the doors open, my tears stop. I refuse to look back. I wipe the tears from my face resolutely and smile at the poor sucker who got on the elevator on the thirteenth floor. I square my shoulders and walk through the lobby and out into the Chicago sunshine. I stop and take a huge deep breath. "Everything's going to be all right, Cassandra," I say to myself. Words my dad used to say run through my head. *No matter how bad things get, it will always get better.*

I walk a few blocks to breathe in more fresh air. When I get to the bus stop, I hop on the metro bus en route to my home. Inside the door, I set the box down, strip out of my outfit, and plop my ass on the couch in my bra and panties. "It's time to regroup," I say to the walls. And I *will*. Tomorrow.

7

DAVID

YOU KNOW THAT MOMENT? THE ONE WHEN YOU REALIZE YOU JUST FUCKED UP THE BEST THING TO EVER HAPPEN TO YOU AND SHE DID NOTHING TO DESERVE IT AND SHE AIN'T COMING BACK? YEAH, WELL IT SUCKS.

"I just stood there."

"You just stood there?" my sister Sandy asks. Her disbelief and disappointment in me radiate from the phone's speaker.

"Yeah, I just stood there. I watched her grab her box of stuff and walk down the hallway."

"Why?"

"Why what?" I spit defensively.

"Why did you let her walk away? Why didn't you stand up for her?"

"I. Don't. Know! It's complicated!" I shout. I can't explain to my sister that I diddled my assistant in a dirty fucking alley outside of Emmit's and that I liked it but I regretted it too. To be honest, I'm even a bigger shit than Sandy thinks, because when Lester said she was going back to the pool, I felt a twinge of relief. I had the instant thought that it would be easier for me if she were gone, because it was just going to be awkward as fuck now to work together. I told myself that since it was Lester's decision, I was off the hook. But I know that's complete and utter bullshit.

"Jesus, Dave. If you can't talk to me like a normal person instead of a raging douchebag, I'm hanging up. Maybe it's better for Cass to be rid of you. She doesn't deserve to be treated so horribly. You are truly an asshole. God, this pisses me off. Fuck you, Dave! I'm hanging up."

The phone clicks as she follows through with her threat. My sister hung up on me. I sigh as I hit the End button on my phone. It has taken a few months to get back in her good graces after my wife and I split. My wife, now ex-wife, treated her like shit. I knew it at the time, but I let it happen, and she was understandably furious with me. Since the divorce, I've apologized profusely and begged for forgiveness, which she did with some caveats. Obviously, I've taken a giant step backward toward the glacial abyss I'd been in for months with this latest fuckup, at least as far as my sister is concerned.

Before I married Jennifer, Sandy and I'd always been tight. She's always been my confidant. Before Jen, Sandy and I told each other everything. You'd think, as a guy, I'd be closer to my brothers and would confide in them, but they don't get me like Sandy gets me. Sandy also doesn't put up with my bullshit, unlike Cassie. No, *she* put up with my bullshit on a daily basis. I'm pretty sure Cassie recognized when I was giving her bullshit; she just didn't call me out on it. She let me get away with it. She was always professional.

I pick up my phone to text Sandy.

Me: Sorry.
Sandy: Whatever, asshat. You're a fucking VP. Request the assistant you want. Bring her back from that damn pool.
Me: I guess.
Sandy: Seriously, grow a pair. Did you even ask if they cut her pay?

Shit. I didn't think of that. She already lives in a rat-infested hellhole.

Me: I'll check.
Sandy: Jesus, dude. GROW. A. PAIR.
Me: Yeah. Okay.

I'm turned in my new chair, staring out at the city. I sighed. "Sandy's right, I won't get anything done without Cass." I turn the chair to face my desk and log in to my schedule. Gretchen has updated it for the day. She even scheduled me to spend lunch with her today. The entry says, "Get to know Gretchen." As I click on the entry to delete it, she appears in my doorway.

"Dave? Did you see I scheduled lunch together?"

"Uh-huh."

"I thought we'd order in. Have a cozy lunch here on your sofa."

"Uh-huh."

"What do you want to eat?" she says with a smirk.

Not you. "Reuben, fries, and sweet tea," I say in a monotone voice.

"All right. I'll get lunch and see you back here shortly."

She turns and saunters away from me, doing her damn best to make those narrow, manly hips sway. "Not gonna happen, sweetheart," I mumble to myself. "You've got to have real womanly hips like Cassandra's to make that work." I turn to look at my screen and think about what Sandy just said. Before I talk to Lester about Cassie, I text Cassie to see how she's doing.

Me: Cassie, it's me, David. Are you okay?

I wait for a while, minutes, just staring at my phone.

Cass: I'm fine.
Me: I'm sorry.
Cass: It's fine.
Me: What was I supposed to do?
Cass: Grow a pair.

Has she been talking to Sandy?

Me: Ha-ha. You know I've got a pair. ;)

I wait for a few minutes, but she doesn't text back. She must have gotten busy. Lester said she'd have a lot of work to do.

I pick up my phone to call Janice in the administrative assistant pool.

"Hello?"

"Yes, hello, Janice. This is David Flynn. How are you today?"

"Good. Congrats on your promotion. You deserve it."

"Oh, thanks."

"What can I do you for?" she asks. She's all business now.

"I'm checking on Cassandra."

"Cassandra Darrow?"

"Yeah. Is she okay? Is she going to get a pay cut now that she's back in the pool?" I know that's none of my business, but I need to know.

"Well, if she was still employed by IIM, I wouldn't be able to answer you. Since she quit, I can tell you she would have received a substantial cut in pay if she had gone back to the pool."

Fuck! "What do you mean she quit?"

"I mean, she quit. She emailed me this morning to tell me she quit. To be honest, I don't blame her. If you'll excuse me saying so, Mr. Flynn, sending her back to the pool was pretty bad form."

Fuck! I'm Mr. Flynn now? I ignore her comments—what could I say in my own defense? "Okay. Thank you very much, Janice."

"You're welcome."

I have an old habit of always listening for the other person to hang up. So, I wait. When I don't hear the click, I say, "Hello?"

I hear her clear her throat a little. When she speaks again, her voice is low. I can barely hear her. "I probably shouldn't say anything, but I feel like I need to warn you."

"Warn me?"

"Gretchen has a thing for the vice presidents, and it never ends well for the VP. Sexual harassment accusations. That's why there was an opening for you to fill." I stopped to think for a second. I'd heard rumors that the last VP stepped down after a sexual harassment complaint had been registered against him.

"What did Gretchen have to do with that?"

"Well... she's Lester's niece, so there's that. Not to mention, she's a piece of work."

Fuck! "I didn't know that."

"Now you do. Talk to you later."

I wait to hear the click again. Once I do, I hang up my phone. Placing my head in my hand, I groan. "This is so fucked up."

"Oh, now, things aren't that bad, are they?" Gretchen's voice is syrupy sweet, and I hate it.

I look up and see her setting out our meals. I mentally cringe because I'm just noticing that she looks like my ex-wife,

Jennifer. In spite of myself, I shudder and glance away from her. When I look back, she pats the seat next to her on the sofa, but I ignore her. I move to the seating area but sit in the side chair. Grabbing my food, I say nothing. I'm not in the mood to talk. I'm hungry. And pissed. And disgusted with myself. Absolutely fucking *disgusted* with myself.

8

DAVID

I HATE MY JOB.

The first two weeks at my new job has sucked balls. I hate my new ergonomic chair. I hate the view, and I really, truly hate my new assistant. She knows nothing, absolutely nothing, about this business. Hell, she barely knows how to spell. I have to proofread my own fucking memos after she types them. I'm scared shitless she's sent some letters out to clients with my name on them that I haven't seen and corrected—because I'll be humiliated if she has. Couple her ignorance of our business with her constant need to touch me, and you get an inkling of the hell I'm in.

Fact: If she gets within two feet of me, some part of her is touching some part of me—like one long, talon-like fingernail scraping down the top of my hand or how about her sliding so close to me that her breast brushes against my arm. Then there was last Tuesday. That day she "accidentally" spilled a bottle of water in my lap and then attempted to clean me off with her bare hand. When that happened, I jumped out of my fucking ergonomic chair and said, "Enough, Gretchen! Do *not* touch me." I walked into my bathroom, slammed the door shut and locked it. Glaring at myself in the mirror, I muttered, "If she accused someone of sexual harassment, it's just plain bullshit. It's like she's got fucking tentacles," I grumble. Part of me wants her to get caught at her own game; the other part of me sincerely knows *I* would get fired.

That last thought stops me short. How is it that, in less than two weeks, I went from loving my job to hating everything about it? I already know the answer to my question, but I can't say her name. *Cassandra*. Shit, I thought it—I didn't say it. In my first two weeks as vice president, I've accomplished nothing, and I mean *nothing*. Not since she left. Lester has had me in his office four times to ask me what deals I've got brewing. I didn't have the balls to tell him the truth. The truth is that, without Cassie, I have nothing brewing. No new ideas. Nothing.

Maybe I should call her. I could ask her to dinner, see how she's holding up. If she hasn't found a job yet, I could make some calls on her behalf. "Yeah, that's a great idea." I pull the phone out of my pocket and hit her number. It goes to voice mail, so I leave a message. "Cassie, hey, it's David. I'm calling to see how you're doing and ask if you'd like to have dinner with me this week. I've, uh, missed you. So, yeah, call me." I hang up and stare at my phone. "Jesus, I sound like a pathetic ass. But if it gets her to call me back, then it's worth it." I wince. I've gotta quit talking to myself, but I feel like I've just done something proactive; I feel energized after making the call. I square my shoulders and spin my chair around to my computer and get to work. I've got client investments to monitor and a staff to manage. Being a vice president isn't all fun and games after all.

My next plan is to keep Gretchen busy doing mindless shit. Take now, for example. I've got her busy reorganizing my files. It was probably a mistake, who knows how she'll do it, but I had to think of something to keep her out of my office. By four o'clock, Cassie still hasn't returned my call. "Maybe she's already got a new job." I hope so. I would hate for her to lose the shithole she's living in and be forced to live somewhere even more terrible. I shiver recalling her apartment. I only visited her once to drop off some papers, and I was shocked to see the state of her neighborhood and the exterior of her building. I was surprised, however, to see how pristine her tiny, efficiency apartment was. She'd taken lemons and made lemonade, as they say. The place was decorated in soft pastel colors. It looked cozy. Comfortable.

At 5:00 p.m., there's still no call, so I grab my coat and head out the door. "I'm beat," I mumble to myself in the elevator. It seems funny to be this tired; I actually did nothing more than check on clients and surf the internet for the best deal on fishing gear. I don't know why I did that—I don't even fish. At home, I change into sweats and an old University of Illinois tee. I plop my ass on the couch and speed-dial the pizza place around the corner. I love the Chicago-style pizza from this place. I order a large Beast Master with extra cheese. My mouth starts to water, anticipating the pizza topped with every kind of meat and vegetable along with a mixture of four different cheeses: Mozzarella, white cheddar, pepper jack, and provolone. It's damn good. Cassie loves it too, but whenever I ordered it in, she'd eat one slice while I ate the rest.

Resting my feet on my coffee table, I grab the remote, scrolling through the channels. The Cubs are playing, but I feel like watching a movie. I've got numerous movie channels, so I search through them looking for something I've never seen. "I feel like watching something old or a classic." Shit, I've got to stop talking to myself. Cassie was right; I sound like a crazy person when I do it. I finally find one about an English woman named Bridget something or other. It says it's a comedy, so I'll try it. Five minutes in and I know I've stumbled on a chick flick, but it's made me chuckle already, and I could sure use a laugh. My doorbell rings. "Pizza time," I say to myself. Once I'm planted back onto my sofa, beer in hand, I sigh. I'm halfway through the film when I wonder why Sandy never made me watch this. It's her kind of movie. It sucks watching it alone. Hell, everything sucks right now. Ever since... No, I can't think about Cassie right now. Whenever I do, it makes me agitated, tense. She was my calming force. Now that she's gone... I pick up my phone to send Sandy a text to invite her over when it rings. Cassie's name appears on the screen. I stop the movie and answer as fast as I can, "Hello?"

There's a pause before she speaks, "Oh, hi, David. I heard your message." She pauses again, "Um, how are you?"

Hearing her voice makes me smile. I feel suddenly better. "I'm good. What have you been up to? Did you find another job?"

"No. Not yet. I'm taking my time. I want to be sure it's the right fit."

The right fit? What does that mean? "Sure. That's a good plan. So, um, do you want to go out with me? Dinner?"

"Oh," she pauses. "Yeah, sure. When?" Cassie's voice sounds a little distant.

"I've got a thing on Friday, so what about Thursday?"

"Thursday works. Shall I meet you somewhere?"

"That's a good idea. I'll book us a table at Next. Seven o'clock?"

"Next? I've heard that place is fantastic. It sounds wonderful. See you then." She sounds a little more herself now, and I feel relief. Maybe she'll forgive me for not speaking up for her.

"It's a date!" I say happily. I'm smiling from ear to ear when I hang up. I'm going to see Cassie! I need to see her and talk to her again, so I can discuss my anxiety about the new job. She can help me ease into this new job and new life as a vice president. She always has good advice.

9

CASSANDRA

NEVER CONFUSE BEING LOVED AND NEEDED: WITH BEING USED AND WANTED.

I'm so nervous for this date. I've dreamed about him taking me on a real date, but I never thought it would actually happen. Maybe spending two weeks without me has made him see how much he needs me. Or maybe our little tryst in the alley caused him to see something more. Standing in front of my closet, I stare at my clothes. What does one wear on a date with the man of their dreams? "Nothing that I already own, that's for sure." That's why I went to my favorite boutique. They've got a wide range of clothing in plus sizes for all occasions, from casual wear to formal gowns. I opted for a stunning cocktail dress in a deep green that goes well with my dark brown hair and green eyes. The fabric is crepe, which is very forgiving for women with problem areas. It's an off-the-shoulder dress fitted from the bodice down to just below my knees. I wasn't sure I could pull off the look, but I have decent shoulders, and the sales woman was encouraging, so I felt emboldened to buy it.

I bought a new pair of shoes too—open-toed, nude sling backs with a few crystals on the top and sides that create some sparkle. I fell in love with the shoes, but I spent way too much on them. They cost nearly twice as much as the dress, but I justified the purchase by promising myself I'd wear the shoes a lot more than the dress. I decide to wear my hair down and apply a little makeup. I dab on some of my favorite perfume and finish the look with simple earrings, a cuff bracelet, and red lipstick. I smile at myself in the mirror. "Not bad, Cassie. Not bad." I just hope David thinks so too. Grabbing my clutch, I toss in the necessities and open my front door. Outside, I hail a taxi; it's an easy trip. The majority of the route is straight down Halstead. I make it to the restaurant with five minutes to spare.

The minute I step inside, I gasp at the interior of the restaurant. Next is, in a word, sexy. The lights are dim but not so dim that I can't see the clean lines of the interior. Each table on this level seems like its own tiny, private oasis. My fascinated perusal of the interior design is interrupted when the beautiful hostess asks, "May I help you, ma'am?"

Ma'am? I hate that. I'm not a ma'am yet. But I smile anyway and say, "I'm meeting my date here. David Flynn?"

Her eyes pop open a little too quickly. No doubt she's surprised that David is my date. "Follow me. He's right this way." I follow the little pixie of a woman until she stops at a table and raises her palm.

My eyes follow her hand. I see him and smile. When our eyes meet, he stands. I release the air from my lungs at the sight of him. My smile brightens because, dang it, I've missed him. The last two weeks without seeing him have been hard. "Cassie," he whispers, leaning down. After kissing my cheek, he reaches out and puts his hand on my back, guiding me to my chair. "You look beautiful."

"So do you." David in a suit and tie is a sight to behold—it makes me a little weak in the knees. Tonight, he's wearing a suit I've never seen. The fabric is charcoal-colored with a subtle windowpane pattern in the fabric. He's paired it with a plaid shirt in soft grays and blues, and he's finished the look with a deep blue tie. He looks like he shaved after work. His usual five o'clock shadow is gone. Instead, his face is smooth and sculpted. He's gorgeous.

He smiles a little tentatively. "Have you ever been here? I chose it because it's close to your place. Did you have any difficulty finding it?"

I'm a little puzzled. The restaurant isn't that close to my place, but I let his comment pass. I smirk at him; does he think I've had a slew of sexy dates here? "No, I've never been here. I read about it after we talked, and the reviews are great."

"It has been getting good reviews." He clears his throat a little.

Is he as nervous as I am? If so, I can't help finding that rather sweet. Our server arrives just then to take the drink order. David orders a top shelf whiskey, and I order white wine. I return to his question. "I've been good." I want to say, "I've missed you," but instead I continue, "How have you been?"

"Good," he says a little too loudly. He lowers his voice. "Good. Fine."

"Are you spending too much time looking out your window?" I giggle.

He chuckles. "I am. You were right. I can't help myself."

The waiter brings our drinks and tells us he will give us a few more minutes to look at the menu. I pick up the leather-bound menu and busy myself, appearing to study it. In reality, I'm dreaming about the amazing time I'm having. I'm also wondering if we'll go somewhere after this. Dancing? David is an excellent dancer. I slowly breathe in and out to calm myself and hastily choose the salmon. It's light and easy, and I'm probably not going to eat much of it anyway. "I think I'll have salmon. What about you?"

"Meat," he rumbles. "If there's beef in it, I'll order that." He chuckles.

Once we place our order, David leans a little closer to me. He's so close I can smell his cologne. Scent can really jog your memory, and his reminds me of the night in the alley—him standing so close to me there's no space between us. I sigh before I can stop myself as I recall those moments. His hand is beneath my skirt—*stop it, Cassie*. I clear my throat and sip my water. I know I've just made myself blush, but hopefully it's dark enough in the restaurant that he won't see it.

He doesn't seem to notice the red blotches that I'm sure have appeared on my neck and face. "So, what have you been doing for two weeks?"

"A little of this and a little of that."

One of his eyebrows rises high up into his forehead. Then his eyebrow relaxes as he leans back in his seat. "What does that mean?"

I'd love to tell him that I've been hard at work looking for another job, but the truth is, I haven't even been looking. I needed a breather. "It means that I've been giving myself some time to think about what I want to do next. I have several options, and I want to be sure I make the right choice. I needed a break; I'll get to work on it next week."

"Sure, I get it. Do you want me to make some calls? I know people at other investment firms who need a good secretary."

"Secretary?" I hate that word. It's archaic, and it has negative connotations in my mind.

"Assistant. You know what I mean."

I give him a small smile. "Of course. No calls needed yet. Thank you for offering, though. I'll let you know if I need anything." *No, I won't.*

He leans forward into my personal space again. "Have you been reading?"

"Reading? Of course. I love reading. I bought a new mystery by Dean K—"

"No, not reading for fun. Have you been reading up on any new businesses, investments, things like that?"

"Oh, some. I can't seem to help myself." I giggle.

I watch as he pulls out a pen from the inside breast pocket of his jacket. Next, he removes a small piece of paper from his hip pocket and sets that on the table. Pen poised over the paper, he asks, "So what did you find out? Anything of interest for me?"

I stare at him. My stomach has flipped and taken a nose dive. I set down my wine glass as the burn of tears behind my eyes rears its ugly head. I refuse to cry. I will be strong—but I won't be silent. "So, let me get this straight, David," I say quietly and as calmly as possible. "You want some investment tips from me?"

"Well, sure, if you've got any." He shrugs nonchalantly.

"You asked me here tonight, not for a date, but for business advice." It's not a question; it's a statement of inevitable truth. I set my napkin on the table and push my chair out to stand.

"What? What's going on? What are you doing, Cass?"

I lean forward with my hands on the table. "I'm leaving." Standing up as tall as someone five feet four inches tall can, and I add, "Goodbye, David. Have a good life." Grasping my clutch, I walk away. From that table. From that man.

I walk briskly to the front of the restaurant and out the door into the crisp night air. Fall is almost upon us, I think irrelevantly. I slip inside the taxi in front of the building and give the driver my address. Then... I let the tears fall. I cry until the taxi pulls up to my front door. That's how long I'm giving myself to cry. I dry my tears and pay the driver. "No more tears for David Flynn," I promise myself as I exit the taxi. David Flynn doesn't deserve it. David Flynn doesn't deserve *me*.

10

DAVID

SOMETHING WENT WRONG AT SOME POINT.

I don't get it. What did I do wrong? Why did she stand up and leave me sitting alone at this table? I haven't moved since she left five minutes ago. Maybe I should have gone after her. I could have asked her what just happened. Our food was delivered just as I lost sight of her in the foyer. She didn't even eat her dinner, for God's sake. I stare at the food on my plate. The hunger I felt when I walked into this place seems to be gone. I look over at her dinner and nausea, as well as the realization, hits me. "I fucked up. Again." Why didn't I realize what I was doing was wrong? Why didn't I look at this from her perspective? She thought this was a date. I knew it the minute I saw her dress. But that confuses me. Why would she assume it was a date? We've always been friends—just friends.

I cringe as the thought hits me. We did practically fuck in the alley outside of Emmit's. I lean my head back and close my eyes as a wave of insight swamps over me. "Fuck!" I say, sitting straight up. "I called it a date." I called it a fucking date when I asked her to dinner. I lean forward with my elbows on the table and let my head rest in my hands as I squeeze my eyes shut. "I fucked this up so badly, I don't think I'll ever get her back." And I need her. No, not *that* way—well, okay, –I would like another taste of that beauty mark. My thoughts kick into high gear and my fantasies take over. I have to admit there is a part of me that pictures her spread out on my big bed. I see myself unzipping her dress and getting a firsthand look at *all* of her. Her tits, er, breasts that were practically clawing to get out of that snug, green dress. I tried not to notice the fact that my dick went rigid the second I saw her in that pin-up girl outfit. She looked like a bombshell. "Fuck!" I say a little too loudly.

"Sir?" says the hostess. "You're going to need to keep it down. You're disturbing the other customers." She smiles at me coyly. "Do you need anything? Anything at all?" she adds, leaning against my table. Her hips are so small I'm pretty sure my hands would touch if I wrapped them around her. I'd break her like a twig if I ever tried to bed her.

"Can you box these up for me?" I point to both plates. Maybe if I follow her home and bring the food along, I can talk myself out of this situation and into her bed. What the hell? *Talk myself into her bed?* What am I saying? I thought she wasn't my type.

I pay the bill and wait for the food. When the hostess hands me the bag, she also slips a small piece of paper into my breast pocket. Her number. I give her a small smile, and I'm out the door. I know Cass lives close by; I hop into a taxi and give the driver her address. I'm dropped off at the corner and walk back to her apartment building. Standing on the stoop, I search the tenant list for Cassandra's name, but it's not listed. I seem to recall she lived on the second floor. I check out the list for the second floor and press the buzzer for apartment 2C. Nothing happens, so I press 2B. "What?" I hear a male voice through the crackling of the old intercom system.

"Uh, yeah, I'm looking for Cassandra Darrow. Does she—"

"Wrong apartment," the guy mutters, and the line goes dead.

I press 2A, and a woman answers, "Yes?"

"Hey, I'm looking for Cassandra Darrow. Do you know which place is hers?"

"Uh, no."

"She lives on the second floor."

"There's no Cassandra in this building."

"Are you sure? She's a bigger girl."

"She's fat?"

"Yes—I mean, no. She's voluptuous."

The voice snorts on the other end of the intercom. "We've got no fat chicks named Cassandra in this building. Maybe she moved." Click. She hangs up on me too.

"She moved?" When the fuck did she move? I step down off the stoop and wander back to the main road. "Who would know where she lives?" I'd call her, but I doubt she'd pick up the phone. I scroll through my contacts to see if anyone there would know. Mallory's name slides by, and I press the Call button.

"Hello? David Flynn? Why are you calling my cell phone at this hour?"

"It's not even eight o'clock."

"I need my beauty sleep."

"Where does Cassandra live? I need an address."

"Why should I give that to you? Better question... why don't *you* already know her address? She was your assistant and practically your wife for ten years, and you don't know where she lives?"

Wife? "I had the address of her old place."

"She moved out of there like three years ago. Jesus, you're so self-centered."

"Self-centered? What are you talking about?"

"Where do I start? I'd love to tell you, but I need my job.

You'd fire my ass if I told you how I really felt about you." I hear her mutter "jackass" under her breath and know I've fucked the pooch on all of this shit at IIM and with Cassie.

"I'm trying to make things right. Will you give me her address? Please?"

She sighs into the phone. "I will, but if you tell her I gave it to you, I will hurt you."

"I promise. What is it?" I listen as she lists the address. "Are you sure? That's a pretty upscale neighborhood." It's not far from my place.

"I'm sure. You should have been paying better attention to her and the beautiful person she is inside and out. All you ever thought about was what she could do for you." I hear her mutter, "Self-centered asshole," and then the line goes dead.

I have to walk a few blocks until I'm able to grab a cab. I read off the address: "1606 N. Mohawk, please." I watch the city fly by my window, thinking about what Mallory just said to me. What I did tonight was wrong. Okay, not just wrong, it was reprehensible. I was using Cassie. I guess I thought an expensive dinner and a little conversation would bring back my ringer. And that's definitely what she is—a ringer. She was my secret weapon at IIM. She had a knack for discovering the best places to invest money. Every morning, she'd bring me my cup of black coffee, a printout of my schedule, and a stack of the financial sections of all of the major newspapers. If she thought something was worthy of my attention, she'd jot down little notes and symbols in the margins. They reminded me of hobo symbols from the turn of the century. Back then, hoboes placed markings everywhere to help their fellow hoboes find what they needed. The marks were placed on fences, posts, sidewalks, buildings, trestles, and bridge abutments to aid them and others of their kind to find help, to steer them clear of trouble, or lead them to food or a place to sleep.

In Cassie's case, the symbols told me that something she read in the paper could show a high rate of return. If that was the case, her symbol was a car. If something was liquid, she'd draw a raindrop. The bull market was a bull's horn, of course. When a company was worth a buy and hold, it was an outline of a hand. If she thought it would have a return of innovation, like the Alte Frau deal, she'd draw a light bulb. She'd also give me warnings about things we'd already invested in or things to avoid entirely. Whenever I saw a triangle with an explanation point inside, I knew I needed to pay attention. I learned pretty quickly to heed these little gems.

Early on, I ignored her tips, and when I discovered I missed the opportunity to double my bank account from something she'd noted in the Wall Street Journal, I started to take her symbols and doodles seriously. Once I did that, we became a well-oiled machine. She'd find the new ventures and research them while I'd manage my customers and advised them to trust my expertise. Once I started to win, and win big, I became the golden boy of Ingot Investments. We were a great team, Cassie and me. We made a lot of money for the company—together. I was showered with promotions and a lot more money. She moved up the ladder right along with me, making a little more money with each promotion. It was perfect. She never once asked that I give her credit. She liked our system too.

At least I thought she did. Perhaps I'm wrong about that, because when she heard me tell the story about Alte Frau at the office party, I saw disappointment on her face for the first time in ten years. All because I'd stolen her story. She was the one waiting for her doctor. She's the one who reluctantly picked up that magazine. She's the one who pocketed the periodical and brought it to work. She was the one who did all of the background research before she even brought it to my attention. Sure, I took a risk investing my clients' money, but I do that every day. It was *her* win, and it should have been her getting the recognition. But I took it because I *am* a self-centered asshole, just like Mallory said. In a very rare moment of honest insight, I admit I was crazy to think I could handle the new job without her. I think I took her for granted—no, I don't think, I *know* I took her for granted. I used her and then left her to swing in the wind.

When the taxi arrives at her address, I'm shocked at the place. Even in the dark, I can tell this place is nice. *Too nice.* Something doesn't add up. Did she inherit money? Does she have a wealthy man in her life? Maybe she's subletting from someone. Oh, I know! She's got roommates. These places are huge. She's probably got three or four roomies. Yeah, that makes the most sense because these townhouses, in this neighborhood, range in price between $500,000 to over a million dollars, which means *this* place is not in Cassandra Darrow's price range.

I double-check the address and see she lives in C. I walk to her door and knock. When I hear nothing, I knock again. I look to my right and see a button. Pressing it, I hear elegant chimes. "Just a second." I hear her voice getting closer to the door. Before she opens it, she asks, "Who is it?"

Good girl. You never know who's knocking on your door at this time of night. "It's me. David."

There's hesitation, then a groan on the other side of the door.

"Cassie. Please? I brought our dinner. I want to apologize."

"Fine," she mutters. I hear several locks disengage, and I wait for her to open the door wide, but it only opens an inch or so. "Go ahead. Apologize. Then please leave."

"Please, Cass? Let me in." Okay, I'm almost begging. Not my style, but I'll do what I need to do to make this right.

"Fine," she mutters again. She pulls the door open abruptly and stands aside.

I step in, and the first thing I notice is her outfit. Fuck! She's got on a tiny tank top and even tinier shorts. She's in her pajamas ready for bed. Her hair is up in a messy bun. Her makeup is gone. I get a glimpse of her pale skin, all of it, from her face down to her braless tits. Her arms are exposed, and her legs... Jesus there's a lot of leg to see, but it's the first time I notice just how small she stands. I've got to be a foot taller than she is. I feel like I'm towering over her. Not only that, my dick is hard as a stone again. All I can think about is pushing her up against the wall and fucking her brains out—right now. However, the look on her face tells me that's not going to happen. At least not yet. "I brought your dinner," I say, smiling as confidently as I can.

She takes the bag from my hand and moves into her place. I watch her ass swing as she walks up three steps into the main part of the house. I'm not sure which is more beautiful, her ass or this place. "Wow, this place is amazing." I want to ask her who owns it, but I'm afraid she'll tell me it belongs to her wealthy lover or something. I don't need to know that shit.

"Thank you," she says, putting her box of dinner in her refrigerator. She hands me back the bag with my meal still inside.

"You don't want to eat your dinner?" I assumed we could sit down and finish what we started.

"I'm not hungry," she says as she crosses her arms just under her chest, forcing her tits up and out even more.

My dick is going to die a painful death if she doesn't stop doing that shit. "You ate when you got home?" Why am I fixated on this?

She sighs and moves out of the kitchen around the corner into a nice sitting area. There are bookshelves on either side of a gas fireplace. It's too warm yet to have that going, but this room is cozy and decorated in an elegant yet comfortable style. Whoever owns this place must like light colors because most of the furniture is pale with dots of bright color here and there.

"This place is fantastic."

"Thank you," she says as she sits down in an oversized chair. She brings her legs up under her and leans on the left arm of the chair. "Have a seat." I sit down at the end of the sofa closest to her chair as she adds, "Can I get you anything? Water? I don't have any whiskey so...."

"Uh, no thanks." I need a minute. I feel like I don't really know this woman—it's like we're meeting for the first time. It makes me feel unsettled and confused. I look at her face and see how beautiful she is, but I also notice that her eyes are red and puffy. "Were you crying?"

"No," she says, too quickly.

Like a dog with a bone, I don't let it go. "Did I make you cry, Cass?" I lean over the arm of the chair to get a closer look. "Did I make you cry, baby?" Okay, why the fuck did I call her baby? She winces at the endearment. I deserve that wince—she's got a right not to trust me.

"You didn't make me cry. It's allergies."

I reach out and place my hand over hers. She's so warm and soft. I curl my fingers around her wrist and grasp it gently. Pulling her forward, she's out of her chair and standing in front of me. I place my hands on her hips and look up at her. Her breathing has quickened, which is making her breasts heave up and down. It's a glorious sight to behold. So much so I feel my own breath quicken too. "I'm sorry about earlier, Cassandra," I whisper as I slide my palms around her waist. "I was a selfish asshole."

She lets out a snort. "You think?" she adds just as I slide my palms down, beneath the leg openings of her tiny sleep shorts.

She lets out a soft moan. It's then I realize I want to hear that moan again, only louder—like the ones in the alley.

"You're not wearing panties."

"Not to bed," she says, panting slightly.

"You're a naughty girl, Cassie."

"Uh-huh," she says absently. I've moved my right hand up to the edge of her shorts, ready to pull them down. I look up at her for permission. "We shouldn't," she says quietly.

"But you want to? Because I know I want to. Look what you do to me, honey."

She peeks down and sees the giant tent in my slacks. She nods, and I move so fast she doesn't have time to change her mind. Her shorts are on the floor in seconds. I look at her pussy and see it weeping. I pull her closer to me, so I can place my nose on her bare mound. I'm a little surprised to see her shaved there. It must be the craze today. Most women are shaved completely bare, and Cassie is no exception. Honestly, I don't care what her pussy looks like, as long as it's dripping wet for me.

"Open your legs for me, Cass." She steps first one leg, then the other out, until she's nearly straddling my legs. I bring my palm up and slide it between her legs. I move her wetness around until I feel her hard, little clit peeking out into the open. "Gorgeous," I mutter.

Leaning forward, I swipe my tongue out until I feel the nub. I run my tongue around in circles, and then I suck it into my mouth. Cassie gasps so loud I can feel it on my tongue. I press my finger into her opening as I suck. Her hips begin to move with me as I fingerfuck her. I can't wait to really fuck her. Damn, she's tight. But there's no way we'll do anything else until she comes. I won't leave her wanting like I did last time.

Fuck! The noises she's making are driving me crazy. There are whimpers and panting. When she grasps my hair and pulls me closer, I latch onto her pussy with my mouth like she's giving me my life source. I feel her before I hear her. My finger is being squeezed so hard I don't think I can pull it out.

Her clit is pulsing against my mouth, and I hear her cuss for the first time. "Fuck yes. Jesus." She lets go of my hair, and I pull away. I look up at her and smirk. "I owed you one."

I think that was the wrong thing to say because she backs up and pulls her shorts up almost as fast as I got them down. "Well, thanks for that, I guess." Turning away from me, she marches back out toward her kitchen.

"You guess?" *She guesses?* What the hell did I do wrong now?

11

CASSANDRA

I HAVE A SIMPLE RULE FOR EVERYONE... IF YOU DO ME WRONG, SHAME ON YOU.

Ugh, I let him do me wrong—twice. I guess I'll never learn. After pulling up my shorts, I turn and walk back into the kitchen. I pick up the bag with his dinner inside and walk down to the front door and wait. I can't think of any other way to give him the hint that it's time for him to leave. Sure, I could say, "Get out, asshat." Or "Thank you for coming. Oh, wait, that was me!" or I could just tell him that I'm done with whatever this is and I'd like him to leave. But I opt for the more visual response.

I don't have to wait long. I watch him look for me as soon as he walks into the kitchen. His eyes scan the room until he sees me standing by the door. He takes a deep breath with a look of resignation on his face. At the top of the stairs, he almost drags his feet as he steps down. I reach for the doorknob, but he stops me by placing his big hand on top of mine. "This isn't over, Cassie." He leans down and kisses me softly.

I pull away before the kiss gets out of hand. "Yeah, it is." I pull open the door despite his grip, hold out his dinner, and wait for him to leave. He stares into my eyes for a second; then his eyes slowly scan down my body. My nipples peak as soon as his eyes reach my breasts. Frigging traitors.

He finishes checking me out from head to toe; then he leans in and whispers in my ear, "No. No, it's not, baby. I'll see you real soon."

He walks out, and I slam the door behind him. I know he's close enough, so I yell through the door, "Yes. Yes, we are, *baby*." I say "baby" as sarcastically as possible. When I hear him chuckle, I stomp my foot and growl. "Asshole." I hear him chuckle again. I race up the steps into my sitting room and throw myself on the sofa. The damn thing smells like him. "Ugh!" I groan. I'm in so much damn trouble.

12

DAVID

LIFE SUCKS AND THEN IT GETS BETTER AND THEN IT
SUCKS AGAIN AND THEN IT JUST SUCKS.

Whatever sense of superiority and defiance I felt last night when I left Cassie's place has left me—it's gone. Long gone. Friday is kicking my ass—this job is kicking my ass. The minute I walked into my office, I was summoned to Lester's office with the other vice presidents. The meeting was brief, but it packed a punch. We've all been given a heads-up that we've got to produce something major in the next three weeks, or he's going to rethink the hierarchy at IIM. Lester barked, "The individual directors below you are taking bigger risks and making more money than the lot of you combined. If I don't see something from each of you soon, the shit's gonna get real."

I'd love to laugh at that last statement, because hearing a guy in his late sixties say "shit's gonna get real" is hilarious. The man doesn't scare me. Hell, I could land one punch on him, and he'd be dead; he's so fragile. But the truth is, he doesn't have to use physical force to "get real." Firing us only takes a couple of words and a phone call to Human Resources.

After the meeting, I drag my ass back into my office. Gretchen is at her post, but she's not working. No, she's texting someone. I say nothing. I'd rather have her texting than doing any work for me. She makes my job harder, not easier. Leaving my door ajar, I take my jacket off and hang it over the back of my stupid ergonomic chair. I plop my ass down and spin, so I can stare out the window. The view is nice, sure, but I'd rather be anywhere else right now. I sigh and force myself to face the computer. I click on a few of my standard links, and then I look at some articles on business websites. I also look at local and national news until it's finally lunchtime. "Great, I can get the fuck out of here," I mutter to myself. I stand to pull on my jacket when I hear them—female voices that sound more like hissing cats outside my window at night. "Fuck," I mutter. I stop to listen.

"Where's the other fat one?" says my ex-wife, Jennifer.

"The *other* fat one?" screeches Gretchen.

"Yeah, the *other* fat one besides you."

"You bitch!" shouts Gretchen.

I hear things tumbling and crashing. I stomp out of my office and see Jennifer and Gretchen reaching for each other. "Stop!" I shout. "What the hell's going on here?"

Before I can blink, both women have straightened their hair and clothes and are turning to me with huge fake smiles that are almost identical. It's chilling, like a scene from the Stepford Wives. "Darling." Jennifer walks to me and wraps her arms around my neck. "Darling." She repeats. "I've missed you so much. I came to take you to lunch," she adds cheerily.

Gretchen sneers and grunts as she sits back down. I watch her pick up the items on her desk that were upturned during their altercation. I gently push my ex-wife away. "Jen. What are you doing here?"

She lets out a fake laugh. "I just told you, silly. Let's go into your office so we can be alone," she whispers conspiratorially.

Rather than make a scene, I step back into my office. I wait for her to cross the threshold, feeling like I'm inviting a vampire into my home. I shut the door behind her and stare at her back. "Why are you here, Jennifer?"

She sits on my leather sofa and crosses her long legs. She's wearing an extremely short, tight black dress that hugs her slim figure. Her hair is up in some kind of complicated thing that I'm sure she paid to have done. Her nails are long and bright red to match her lips and her shoes. She's got on too much makeup and perfume. I feel the need to cough because the scent is so thick.

"Well," she says, adjusting her skirt by pulling it up further on her thigh, "I heard you were promoted. I came to congratulate you." She smiles at me prettily, and the smile looks sincere, but I know her and I know that smile is fake as fuck.

"Thanks. You could have texted, sent an email, or better yet, a card."

She fake giggles. "You are so funny, sweetie. I miss that." I watch her expression change from a smile into an expression that would look normal on a sad puppy. The woman is a piece of work. Why didn't I ever see it?

"So, where's Cathy?"

There's one thing that is quintessentially Jen. If she doesn't like you, she calls you by the wrong name. Therefore, she is actually talking about Cassie. "Cassie?"

"Yeah, the fat one."

That's another thing. She thinks it's okay to talk about other women like that. She's been repeatedly cruel to Hank's wife, Sophie, and Mick's wife, Veronica. It's like she feels threatened by them. "Why do you do that?"

"Do what?" she says, looking innocent.

"Make fun of women who are larger than you."

"Well, *hon*, that would be almost all women." She giggles. Letting out a sigh, she adds, "Oh, I don't know. It just disgusts me to see hot men chase chubby girls. I mean, those women don't care enough about themselves to exercise or eat right—

they don't *deserve* a man." She checks her nails like she's telling me something that is so self-evident that she shouldn't have to explain it to me or to anyone.

"You don't exercise." In the two and a half years we were together, she never exercised. Not once.

She giggles again, and the sound makes me feel sick. "That's because I don't need to, silly. I'm naturally thin and beautiful. I don't even have to work at it."

Yeah, if you can describe spending over a grand a month at salons as "not working at it," then I guess she's right. I let out a snort.

"You're laughing at me?" she spits.

"No, not *at* you." Yeah, I'm laughing at her.

It flies right over her head, so she returns to something she understands. "Anyway, I thought I'd take you to lunch to celebrate your big promotion and that huge deal you just landed."

And there it is. The true reason she's here. Somehow, she heard about the money from the Alte Frau investments, and she wants a piece of the wad of cash she thinks is there. "That money came in after the divorce was final, Jen."

"How convenient. I hope you have the documents to prove that."

"I do." At least I think I do. I think Cassie took care of that.

"Because—" She sighs. "—my attorney told me that even if that investment hadn't paid off yet, I'm still entitled to half of it because you risked money that was half mine to get it."

Bullshit! "*My* attorney," I say, "says that's complete bullshit."

"So, you planned that? You planned on waiting until the divorce was final to get that payout?"

"It doesn't work that way. I had no control over the end result until the day the product went on the market."

"Hmm," she says, standing. "We'll see about that. I guess I'll either see you at my attorney's office or in court." She waves with just her fingers adding, "Toodles," as she leaves my office.

"God. Why do you hate me?" I say, looking up toward heaven.

I pull my jacket off and grab my gym bag out of the closet. I open the door to my office. Gretchen scowls at me. "Sorry about her," I mumble. What else can I say? "I'm going down to work out over lunch. Back in an hour or so."

She smiles up at me and nods. "See you then."

13

DAVID

STALKING IS WHEN TWO PEOPLE GO FOR A LONG ROMANTIC WALK TOGETHER, BUT ONLY ONE OF THEM KNOWS ABOUT IT.

The water sluicing down my body feels amazing. My workout was intense and painful—something I badly needed. I feel pain in my arms and legs, and my abs are sore from overwork, but I feel a little like my old self again. I've neglected my workouts, and for me, exercise is a way to center myself. I scrub the sweat out of my hair and work the suds down my chest and stomach. When I reach my dick, I'm tempted to rub one out, but I'd have to think about Cassie to make that happen. She's the only one making my dick hard these days. The thought of her taste on my tongue last night is making me question my decision to jack off. I can almost smell her arousal. "So sweet," I murmur as I wrap my hand around myself.

I think of the moment I pulled her shorts down. The sight of her sweet little pussy drives me onward. I don't know what I expected. Just because she's a bigger girl, I guess I half expected she'd look different down there, but her pussy was small and pink and fucking tantalizing. I pull on myself so hard my head swims. As I'm about to get into a rhythm, I hear a noise. I turn in the shower, still clutching my hard-on, and who do I see standing in my bathroom staring at my cock? "Gretchen!" I shout. "Get the fuck out of here."

"Why?" she says in a husky voice. "It looks like you need a little help there. Not even *your* hand is big enough to handle you."

"Get. Out!" With my teeth clenched, I attempt to speak slowly, so she will understand. I turn off the water because this shower is over. I need a towel, but it's over near the sink.

She giggles and brushes her hands over her own breasts. "You're one hot man, David Flynn."

I do my best to cover myself. My dick went limp the second I spotted her, so that makes it easier to hide myself from her. "How did you get in here?" *I know I locked the door.* She holds up a key. Smirking, she leans her hip against the sink, fondling my towel. I concentrate on my breathing in an attempt to calm myself. "Please go. Let me have some privacy, Gretchen. Please." For the love of God, *please.*

"Oh, all right!" she huffs as she stomps out the door, leaving it ajar.

I rush out of the shower and nearly fall on my ass on the slippery floor. Grasping at the towel, I wrap it around my waist hurriedly. I reach for the door and press the lock button, knowing damn well it won't really do any good if she's got a fucking key. I dry off quickly. "What the hell am I going to do about her?" I'd love to know what happened with Fleming, the last guy in this position. Is this the kind of shit Gretchen pulled on him? I dress in my suit pants, dress shirt, and tie. I walk into my office and cross to the door to close and lock it. I'm sure she's got a key to this door too. At least I'll hear her coming when she tries to enter the office. I pull out my cell and punch in the number for the H.R. assistant director, Jamie Corning. She and I get along well. Maybe she can tell me something about

Fleming or Gretchen. When she picks up, I whisper, "Jamie? It's David Flynn. Are you alone?"

"David? Are you whispering? Ooh, sounds clandestine." She laughs. She's married with, like, twenty kids or something, so she's too tired to be serious. At least that's how she tells it.

"In a way, it is," I whisper into my phone. I don't know if my office is bugged or anything. Yeah, I'm paranoid. "It's about Gretchen."

She groans on the phone. "Yeah? I can't say much about that subject for several reasons."

"She just broke into my bathroom while I was in the shower. She's got a key."

"She did? Christ on a cracker. Do you want to file a formal complaint?"

"Will that do any good?"

"Probably not." She pauses, but I can hear her tapping something in the background. "Okay, let's do this.... I'll make a detailed note about this conversation and put it in your file. I'll keep it in my office until you're ready for it. That will give you a foot to stand on if something goes down." She pauses. "And, David?"

"Yeah?"

"Something *will* go down. That's all I can say. Document *everything* she does that makes you feel uncomfortable. Note dates and times. Got it?"

"Got it."

"Document everything. But not on your work computer. Do it in writing on something you keep with you in your pocket. Don't leave it at work. Do. You. Understand?"

Jesus, what kind of crap did Fleming endure? "Yes. I. Understand," I say, monotone, sounding like a robot.

She chuckles. "Good. Talk to you later. I'll make a note of

this conversation, and you do the same. Remember, note the date and time."

"Will do. Thanks, Jamie."

"You're welcome." I hear her hang up; then I do the same.

I work the rest of the afternoon without interruption until 4:15 p.m. When there's a knock on the door, I groan to myself but say, "Come in." The doorknob jiggles, but it doesn't disengage. I start to stand when I hear a key in the lock. The door opens, and I blink at the sight of my big brother, Hank. Gretchen is gaping at him as she pulls her key from my door. He smirks at her, but as he passes the door, he slams it shut.

"What's with her?" Hank says, pointing his thumb back toward the door.

"My assistant."

"What? Where's Classy Cassie?" He's always called her that, and she always giggled when he said it to her, and it *always* pissed me off that he was so flirty with my girl—er, my assistant.

"She quit."

"What? No fucking way, dude. She'd never leave you. She was in love with you, man."

"Nah, we were friends. A good team, but—"

"I call bullshit, Davie. She was mad for ya. Why'd she quit? And don't lie to me. I can always tell when you're full of shit."

I move out from behind my desk and throw myself in the lone side chair. "I had to let her go. Lester, uh, Mr. Ingot... Gretchen's his niece."

"So? You and I both know you need Cassie."

"I do. But what was I supposed to do?"

"Tell that old fucker that you need your assistant. Pawn his family off on someone else."

I nod. I know Hank is right. If I'd insisted on having Cassie with me, Lester would have eventually folded. But, being the pussy that I am, I'm the one who folded. "That's not all."

"What?"

"I'm nearly positive Gretchen got the last VP fired for sexual harassment."

"She is attractive. Not my type, but you know, she's your type, I guess. If you use Jen as the example."

"Please don't. Neither Gretchen or Jen are my type. Not anymore."

"Are you sexually harassing her? Is that what you're worried about?"

"No, the opposite. She's always fucking touching me. Three hours ago, she used her master key to come into the bathroom while I was in the shower. I had my hands full, if you know what I mean. She wouldn't leave. She offered to help me out."

"Fuck. That's stalker bullshit right there. What are you going to do?"

"Document everything. What else can I do?"

"Too bad you don't have this placed wired up. Cameras, bugs."

"That *is* too bad. I could catch her pulling her bullshit. I'd be protected." That is until Lester decides to fire me for entrapping her.

"Maybe. Most likely you'd have to go if she's Lester's kin. But at least you'd go out innocent. Try to get a new job with a sexual harassment accusation hanging over your head."

"True, brother. Very true."

"I'll hook you up. I've got some surveillance stuff in my car. As long as I get it back, I'll let you use it. I'll even set it up. What time is she leaving for the night?"

I look at my watch. "In the next thirty minutes or so."

"Great. I'll be back in thirty. After that's set up, I'll take you out to celebrate your fancy-ass promotion."

"What about Sophie and the kids?"

"They're at Mom's doing some scrapbooking shit about the kids. For me." He rolls his eyes.

Hank's full of crap. He'll love a scrapbook about his kids. He's so head over heels in love with his little family. Everything they do is sunshine and roses. I've got to admit though, Sophie is pretty amazing. "Knock her up again yet?"

"Nah. Working on it." He winks. "It's just a matter of time."

We fist bump as he leaves my office. As I turn to walk back to my desk, Gretchen slithers into my office. "Wow, there are two of you? I'd love to get myself into a Flynn brother sandwich." She laughs.

"There are six of us, actually. Two of those are women."

"I'm not into women, but I wouldn't be shy if there were four of you there. A couple could watch."

"Uh, um... well, why don't you take off for the night? I'm about to head out to meet up with my brother."

"Awesome!" She squeals as she claps. I believe there was some jumping up and down too. "See you Monday!"

"Yep," I say distractedly. I pull out a small spiral notebook that's been sitting in the drawer for at least a year. I open it and jot down the date. I write down my conversation with Jamie, paying particular attention to note the time. I also write, as close to verbatim as I can, what she just said about a "Flynn brother sandwich" and the rest. I shiver thinking about it. "What a creepy fucking woman."

Hank's back before I've finished making notes. He's got a black bag that looks like a medical case and a silver metal briefcase that looks like something James Bond would carry. He sets down the cases and looks around. "The equipment is tiny, so I can set them up in all corners. They'll pick up audio, but the speakers are not super sensitive. So, speak loudly. You can review the footage on your phone. Actually, you'll get a ping if anyone steps in here when you're gone. It's a cool setup."

"Can I put one in my bathroom? Not pointing to the shower but at the door?"

"Probably not a good idea. I can put a bug in there that's hooked up to a digital recorder, so you'll be able to record audio. You can download the files onto your computer if there are any that are pertinent. That's the best way to go. Saves explaining why you're monitoring your own bathroom."

"Good point. You should be a cop." I chuckle. My brother Hank *is* a cop. He's a detective with Chicago P.D. in the homicide division.

"Ha, ha. So, anything happen when I left?"

"She said she wanted to be in the middle of a Flynn brother sandwich."

"Jesus, what a crazy bitch."

"Yeah, when I told her there were four boys, she said she'd let two watch."

"Document that shit, dude. Make sure you write down exactly what she said, along with the date and time."

"Already way ahead of you, brother."

"You need to continue to do that even though you've got these going. It's supporting documentation."

"I will."

I watch him work, and in less than an hour, I've got visuals on my entire office and audio in my bathroom. "Awesome. Now, let's eat. What're you hungry for?"

"Emmit's?" he suggests.

If we go to Emmit's, I'll think about Cassie and the night we were together there recently. "Nah, Let's hit Fado's Pub. Happy hour is still going, and we can get the Pub Burger."

"Perfect. Let's ride." Hank slaps me on the back as we exit my office.

I turn and lock the door, knowing damn well it makes no

fucking difference. "Think I could change my lock without anyone knowing?"

"Doubt it. Maintenance and housekeeping will need to get in there. Plus, there'd be too many questions. Let the devices do their work. Trust me." Hank pushes the down button on the elevator. "When we get to Fado's, we're having a long talk about Cassie."

"Fine." Hank's right. I need to talk about Cassie, and he's just the guy to hear me out.

14

DAVID

I'D LIKE TO SEE YOU. BUT THEN AGAIN, THAT DOESN'T MEAN THAT MUCH TO ME. SO IF I CALL YOU, DON'T MAKE A FUSS. DON'T TELL YOUR FRIENDS ABOUT THE TWO OF US. I'M NOT IN LOVE.

"So, what the fuck's going on with Cassie?" My butt has barely touched the leather of the booth when Hank starts questioning me.

"Can we please order before you start interrogating me? I'm starving, dude."

"Fine." When the waitress arrives, we order our beers and burgers. She takes our menus, and before I can start, he asks again, "What's going on?"

I take a deep breath and tell him everything—from the shit I said at the party to our celebration at Emmit's. I even tell him about the alley.

"That's why we couldn't go to Emmit's? Bad memories?"

"Not bad memories. Just memories."

"Please continue."

See? He's questioning me like a suspect. *I swear, Officer, I didn't kill her*. I chuckle to myself. He didn't hear the joke in my head, but when I look up, he's staring daggers at me. I stared back at him. "Fine. It was amazing."

"What was amazing?"

"She... Cassie. She was amazing. Once I had her in my arms on the dance floor, I nearly came in my pants."

"Were you drunk?"

"Maybe, but that wasn't it. Her smell, her laugh, the fact she's classy. Shit, even her body. She's not my type—"

"Just stop right there. I think Mick and I have both proven that 'type' theory is bullshit. Love doesn't have a 'type.'"

"*Love doesn't have a type?* Jesus, you should print T-shirts with that shit on it. You'd make a mint on the Lifetime Channel."

Hank chuckles. Two seconds later, he slams his fist down on my left hand resting on the tabletop.

"Fuck! Asshole! That hurt."

"You're lucky I didn't do it to your right hand, but it sounds like you need that one quite a bit right now." He bared his teeth at me. "You're welcome. Now, keep talking."

I do as I'm told. I tell him about Cassie and me walking to the new office and meeting Lester and Gretchen. I feel embarrassed and uncomfortable as I describe what Lester said and what I *didn't* say. "She quit that day. She walked out right then, without notice."

"Why would she stay? That would be humiliating to be pushed back down to the bottom after she's worked so hard to get to the top. To get *you* to the top," Hank adds with an arched brow.

"I know."

"You know? Well, I do too. I know for a damn fact she's been the key to your success. I've hung out there and watched her work."

"I know!" I shout. "I know," I repeat more calmly. "I fucked up with her though."

"You mean more than you've just told me?"

"Yeah. I asked her to dinner."

"Finally!" Hank shouts.

Finally what? "I asked her to dinner to see if she had any good leads on possible investments." Hank looks at me blankly. Then he looks at the table, searching for my right hand, but I quickly put it in my lap. Instead, I feel a shooting pain running up my leg. He's jammed his boot into my calf. "Fuck!"

"You lured her to dinner like it was a date and asked her to save your ass?"

"Yes, but I tried to make it up to her," I say quickly. "I went to her place and, um...."

"Um, what?"

"Got her off," I rush through the words.

"Got her off? Made her come?"

"Yeah."

"Then what happened?"

"She kicked me out and told me to leave her alone."

Hank throws his head back and laughs so loud the other patrons stare at our table. "Jesus, you're fucked, dude."

"I know," I say, lowering my head.

"It's not completely a lost cause, though. I think you still have a chance. Do you want another chance with her? Do you want her?"

"She's not my...." I stop as soon as I see his face turn from grinning to pissed. "I'm just getting through a divorce. Oh, by the way, Jen thinks she's going to get half my proceeds from the last deal."

Hank rolls his eyes. "Get your attorney on that and focus on the prize."

"The prize?"

"Cassie, asshole. She's the prize. If you play it right, you could win."

"What are you talking about?"

Hank leans forward in the booth and motions for me to get

closer to him. I'm a little fearful he's going to punch me. My brother, Hank, is big—bigger than me by several inches up and across. He's got muscles that I only dream of getting. The guy is a tank. "You want to win her, little brother—" He pauses for emphasis. "—because you're in love with her."

I sputter and cough. "Bullshit. I'm not in love with Cassie. I'm not in love with anyone." *Only myself.*

"Fine. Be that way. But, mark my words, you love her. Maybe even more than she loves you. If that's the case, you'll need to do a shitload of groveling to get her back. Think about it."

Do I want her back? Yes, I want her as my assistant. Sure, I'd love to fuck her six ways from Sunday. *Sundays... I can see us waking up together on Sunday morning with her snuggled up to me, all warm and soft. We'd mess around in bed for a while, read the paper, and go over the financial section together. We'd get hungry and walk down to Candy's Bakery with our dog to get a Danish.* What the fuck am I thinking? Fuck! There's no way I'm in love. No way!

Hank sits back in his seat and throws his arm over the back of the booth. "It's obvious you're not ready yet. That's okay. When you realize it, call me." He smirks. "You're gonna need a shoulder, man."

I ignore him and say defiantly, "I'm not in love, Henry. Cass and me, we're friends—maybe best friends. Love is supposed to be work. My relationship with her is effortless—at least it was until I fucked it up."

"Yeah, man. It's supposed to feel right. Effortless. Not that dealing with a woman is easy. It isn't, but the connection you feel is effortless. At least that's how it feels when you've got a real woman. A real woman cares more for her man and her kids than she does about herself. The best thing you can give her is the same back, man. Love her like she's the world to you. If you do that, your rewards will be endless."

Christ, when did Hank get all romantic and shit? It's a little strange. I get what he's saying, not that I've been in a relationship like that, but my folks have it. My mom would do anything for my dad and us. I should use them as my example. Hell, Hank and Mick found it, so I guess it's possible. "I need more beer," I mutter. I can't think about this anymore. One thing I know for sure, though? I'm definitely *not* in love. No way.

15

DAVID

SMILE. YOU'RE ON CAMERA.

The weekend flew by too fast. By Monday morning, all I wanted to do was crawl under the covers and stay there. I don't want to do it. I can't face another week of Gretchen and Lester—another week of failing to come up with any new ideas. For the first time in a decade, I want a different job. I could call in sick. I don't think I've ever taken a sick day. I'm due. I could use the day to meditate. Better yet, I could brainstorm new career options. Maybe Cassie has found something new and different. I could ask her....

No, that's not going to happen. She hasn't returned any of my calls. I called her Friday night after I got home from having dinner with Hank. I called her the next morning to see if she wanted to go get a coffee. On Saturday night, I drank half a bottle of Scotch and left her a drunken message. I remember making the call, I just don't remember what I said. I suspect whatever it was isn't going to win favor with her. On Sunday afternoon, I sent her a text apologizing for the drunken phone message. Like I said, I don't know what I babbled on about; I'm just assuming I needed to apologize. She sent no reply to that text, nor did she call me back. Maybe she's out of town?

I can't seem to shake my melancholy. So, I'm doing it! I'm texting in sick. Call it a mental health day. I send a text to Gretchen, letting her know I won't be in today and to reschedule my meetings for tomorrow. She writes back asking me the following series of questions: 1) Are you ill or are you in meetings somewhere? 2) If you are ill, do you need me to make you an appointment with your doctor? 3) Should I come to your place and nurse you back to health? And finally, she asks, 4) Is it okay if I leave for the day since you're not here?

"Ugh! I should have gone to work. It would have been easier." I reply 1) No. 2) No! 3) No. 4) No. There, that should take care of it, right?

Wrong.

For the next two hours, I'm inundated with texts, emails, and voice mails from her asking about everything from buying more coffee for the office coffee maker to needing me to sign a purchase order for more printing ink. I finally resign myself to the fact that she's worthless. "Just go home," I say during the tenth phone call. If I had actually been ill, she would have driven me straight to my grave.

She was quick to respond with, "Oh, okay. If you're sure."

"I'm sure. See you tomorrow."

"Oh, you're feeling better? I'm so glad. I hope I helped."

I groan and hang up the phone. I throw my head back and look at my clock. Three thirty already. The day is gone. She even ruined my fucking sick day. When I hear my phone sound, I look over and see the app that Hank installed on my phone come to life. It automatically activates when someone is in my office. It happened twice on Friday night when the cleaning crew worked in the office, but it's been quiet since. Not even Gretchen went in there today.

When I press the app to view the feed, it's not maintenance, and it's not the cleaning crew. It's Lester Ingot. "What's Lester doing in my office?" I watch him as he walks over to my desk and sits in my ergonomic chair. "I fucking hate that chair," I grumble. He presses on my keypad, but I'd shut down my computer on Friday, so it doesn't wake up. Next, he starts to lift papers and opens folders on my desk, careful not to move things around too much. He searches my middle desk drawer, but all I've got in there are pens and office supplies. He opens up the drawer on the left side of my desk and sifts through the stuff in it. There's nothing of interest in that drawer either. I've got some old thumb drives along with brochures from various conferences I've attended. It's really just junk.

He slams that drawer shut and tries to open the lower left drawer. I've got that one locked because that's where I store some of my more high-profile client folders. Much of that information is confidential, so I like to keep it closed and locked. He jiggles the drawer and picks up my letter opener. He's doing his best to jimmy the lock, but he gives up and throws the opener back on my desk. His face looks furious—frustrated. He sits back in my chair and runs his fingers through his hair. He stands and looks through the papers on my desk again. The camera isn't powerful enough to show me what he's looking at; I only see white papers strewn about.

I confess, I don't keep a tidy desk. I like to have all of my papers and research at my fingertips. Sure, I've got to dig for things, but it's my system, and it has worked for me. Cassie knows how to find shit—or she did. I sigh and watch as Lester flips over a couple of folders and then stops. He leans down like he's reading something. Lester pulls out his phone and places it over the papers. He's taking a damn photo. "What the hell are you looking at, Lester?"

Nothing on my desk is good to anyone but me. I've got notes from meetings, old newspapers, printed research on clients and companies, and junk mail—lots and lots of junk mail. He pockets the phone and does a shitty job trying to move the papers back the way he found them. I probably wouldn't have noticed anything out of the ordinary, but now, when I go in tomorrow, I'll look through that shit and try to figure out what he found so goddamn interesting.

16

CASSANDRA

WHEN HIS GENTLE SIDE MAKES YOU WEAK AND HIS DOMINANT SIDE MAKES YOU WET.

Being out of work for almost a month should probably bother me more than it has. I've actually accomplished a great deal. I've had a punch list of sorts since I moved into my place that I've never had a chance to complete. Since quitting IIM, I've crossed off three major items from my list. The first was repainting my bedroom. It was bright red—I shiver just thinking about it. Try sleeping in a room the color of blood. It's not easy. Now, it's a soft blue. I've purchased new bedding and accessories to match. The new hue and home goods make a world of difference. I swear I sleep better than I have in years.

The second item on my list relates to my home office. I tend to let papers like old receipts and invoices pile up. In this case, three years of papers are crammed into shoeboxes, grocery bags, and plastic tubs. I keep everything, even junk mail. It's a bad habit. So, week two of my permanent vacation from IIM was spent sorting through those papers, shredding the papers with confidential information, filing the things I actually needed to keep, and tossing out the junk. Once that was done, I felt a weight lift off my shoulders that I didn't realize had been there. I don't know why I let it get that bad. I vow not to let it go that long. "Once a month." I'll sort through my papers once a month. "Yeah, right." I snort. Like that's ever going to happen.

My third project is one I'm currently working on, and it relates to my career goals. I'm studying up to take my final test in the series of investment securities exams from the National Futures Association. Once this final test is complete, I can get back to work and *not* as someone else's assistant this time. No, it's time for me to take the plunge and make my own way—something I've put on hold for seven years. Just as I hit Save and Submit on the exam, I hear a knock at my door. I look down at my watch and note that it's late for visitors, almost 9:00 p.m. I hear another knock then the doorbell chime. I walk down the steps to the door. "Just a second." When I get to the door, I say, "Who is it?"

"David."

Shit! I don't need David Flynn tonight—or ever. "What do you want, David? I'm busy."

"I need to talk to you."

I sigh. "We've got nothing to talk about, David. I was about to go to bed."

"At nine o'clock?"

I ignore that comment, hoping he leaves.

"It's about Beranger Aeronautics."

Beranger Aeronautics? I unlock each of my locks, open the door, and see David Flynn in a pair of workout pants that are hanging low on his narrow hips and a gray Chicago Bears T-shirt that's so snug you can make out the lines on his ripped abdomen. I almost groan aloud when I see him. He hasn't shaved in a few days, and he's in need of a haircut. I used to make his appointments when I saw his hair get too long. I'd add it to his schedule for the day, and he'd go without any argument. We were a good team.

I pull the door open wide enough for him to enter. He steps

past me, giving me a once-over from head to toe as he walks by. I picked the wrong time to wear my yoga pants that are a size too small and a tight white V-neck Loyola tee. Luckily, I'm still wearing a bra. I follow him up my steps into the living room. I motion him toward my little sitting room. "Can I get you anything? Beer? Wine?"

"I'll have a beer, thanks," he says, looking around my place. "Where are your roommates?"

"Roommates?"

"Yeah, I assume you've got roommates in a place like this. What've you got here, three bedrooms?"

"Uh-huh." Why would he assume I have roommates?

"Shit, I didn't even know you'd moved until...."

"Until what?"

"Uh, until I checked on your address. I thought you still lived on the south side."

He knew I'd moved. I took a couple days off to get it done. "Well, you were just starting to see Jennifer. I think you were preoccupied with her." It's the truth.

I watch him pretend to shiver. "Don't remind me. Oh, she came to my office saying she was there to congratulate me."

I let out a snort all while rolling my eyes. The woman is pure vitriol.

"Yeah, that's what I thought too. She wanted to get her hands on the Alte Frau money."

"But that money—"

"Yeah, came in after the divorce was final. My attorney is working on it."

"I hope she doesn't get any of it."

He looks at me curiously. He nods and sits on the sofa. I walk into the kitchen and grab a bottle of beer. I remove a wine glass from my cupboard and pour myself some chardonnay. Back in the sitting room, I hand David his beer.

"So, you live here alone?"

"Yes."

"Are you subletting the place?"

"No."

"You own it?"

"I do."

"But how?"

"How what? You want to know how to go about purchasing a property? Well, first, you hire a real estate agent. Next you—" I begin mockingly.

"Smart-ass," he grumbles. "This place has to be half a million bucks."

"Not that it's any of your business, but it was $725,000. Now, tell me the reason for the visit. What about Beranger Aeronautics." I know he wants more information about my home, but I'm not giving him any.

"Well, about a week ago, Lester was in my office digging through my desk."

"Good luck finding anything on your desk." I chuckle. "You're a slob. Wait. You saw him do it?"

"I wasn't there. My cameras caught him."

"Cameras?"

"Let me start from the beginning." David tells me about Gretchen and his concern about sexual harassment and about Hank and his camera equipment. He pulls his phone out and demonstrates how the app works and even shows me the video of Lester searching through his things.

"Wow! What do you think he was looking for?"

"I wasn't sure. When I went into the office the next day, I carefully looked through the spot he focused on, and the only thing that stood out was the article you gave me about Beranger Aeronautics with your symbols in the margin."

"I remember that article." It was about Beranger going public in advance of the release of new handheld, touch screen computer technology that will give astronauts more freedom of movement in space. When I read about their newest CFO, Chief Executive Officer, my instincts took over. Red flags galore! So, I sketched out two symbols that only David would understand in the margins: the warning sign, or the triangle with the exclamation point inside, and a star with lines trailing behind it to represent a falling star. I don't always think about what I'm doodling in the margins, but the warning sign is one I use a lot.

"I know the man who's now the CFO of Beranger, Alistair Brown, and he's unscrupulous. He used to be one of my professors at Loyola. He quit, or was asked to leave, under mysterious circumstances. We'd heard it had something to do with mishandling of departmental funds, but nothing was ever confirmed," I share. He was also a cruel and angry man that I avoided whenever possible. I refuse to think about the things he said to me. Luckily, I had only one class with him—business ethics, if you can believe that. I turn back to David. "Why do you think Lester is interested in Beranger?"

"I'm not sure. It's a concern, though. I can't shake the feeling I'm about to get set up."

"They're going public day after tomorrow."

He looks at me with an arched brow.

"What? I'm still reading the financial section. I'm not going cold turkey." I laugh.

"What are your thoughts on this new space technology they say they've got?"

"Well, I called a friend of mine who's an aerospace engineer. He'd heard about their claim, and he says it's bogus. Touch screens aren't really feasible because of zero gravity and floating objects on the spacecraft. That's what the falling star represented in the margin. I think they're playing a game. It's best to stay far, far away from them."

"I agree." He smirks at me. "Like I'd ever doubt your research and opinions, Cass."

"So, why do you think you're getting set up? If you aren't investing in Beranger, what could they do to you?"

"I've felt that way for a while, ever since I heard about Fleming and Gretchen."

"What about Fleming?" I've met him a few times. He is a nice man with a sweet wife and a new baby.

"Gretchen got him fired. Claimed he sexually harassed her."

"No way." There's just no way. "Why would anyone believe her?"

David stands and walks over to my fireplace. He picks up a photo of my mom and dad then sets it back down. "She's Lester's niece."

Now it all makes sense. "Oh, I see." I stand up quickly and move into the kitchen.

I feel him behind me as I set my wine glass in the sink. "What do you see?" he says softly behind me.

"I see why he insisted she be your new assistant. How is she?"

His hand moves my hair away from my neck. His breath is hot right below my ear. "Terrible. She's fucking terrible," he mumbles as he leans down to kiss me on that spot. "She can't spell, and she knows nothing about the business." I take a deep breath, knowing he's getting closer to me. He presses himself against my back. "You smell so fucking good, Cassie."

His hand slides around my waist to pull my back snug against his chest. His hard-on presses into my lower back, and I moan before I can stop myself. I lean my head back and look up at him. "This is a bad idea."

"I fucking love bad ideas," he says as he leans down to

capture my mouth with his. It's not a soft kiss either. It's hard and almost angry. "Jesus, I've missed you, Cass."

I turn in his arms and wrap mine around his neck. I say nothing as I press my hard nipples against him and lean in for more. His hands slide down my back, first to cup my ass and then down to my thighs. He pulls me upward until I'm sitting on top of the breakfast bar. His breathing has turned into panting. "I need to be inside you, baby."

I've never seen him like this. I like it. I reach down and pull his shirt up, so I can see his chest. He lifts his arms, grabbing the T-shirt as it reaches his hand, and tosses it to the ground. He then pulls my shirt up over my head. He doesn't pull it free though. He twists and winds it around my wrists until I'm restrained. "Don't move your hands."

He reaches around and unhooks my bra, and I watch his expression change from determination to awe. I've got large breasts, probably bigger than any he's ever seen in person.

"Jesus fucking Chr—" He moans. His mouth is on a breast before he can finish the last word. He moves to the other one while his free hand squeezes and pinches the unattended nipple.

I moan as he uses his tongue and teeth to bring me to life. I wiggle my body in an attempt to get closer to him. I want him all over me. I want to touch him, but my hands are tied, literally. "Untie me," I gasp. "I need to touch you."

He reaches up and untwists and tugs until my shirt is on the floor. He pulls the bra completely off of me and adds it to the growing heap of clothing. I reach into his sweats and grasp his giant cock. "God, you're huge," I whisper.

He pulls my hands away and uses his palm to push me back onto the counter. When I hear a rip, I flinch. He's torn a hole in the crotch of my yoga pants. "Damn it, David. I loved those pa— oh, fuck it," I murmur the second I feel his tongue sweep through my folds. He uses his fingers to pull my labia apart as he licks and sucks until I explode. Not giving me time to recover, he pulls his sweats down to his knees, grabs my hips, and slides me to the edge of the counter. I'm teetering on the edge about to fall when his huge dick starts to slide into me. "Oh God." It feels amazing. I lean back and wrap my legs around him, letting my heels press into his tight ass. "Fuck me, David. Fuck me, please!" I'm lost in him when he thrusts all the way inside.

Planted deep, he leans down so he can whisper in my ear, "I knew you'd feel like this, Cassie. Like fucking heaven." He pulls out and pushes back in so fast I'm nearly launched off the back edge of the breakfast bar. His grip is so tight on my hips; I know there'll be bruises. I don't care. Mark me, please.

Next, I feel myself being pulled. Once I'm on my feet, he turns my body around and presses down on my back. "Bend over and hold on to the edge of the counter."

I hesitate for a moment. I've never done it like this.

"Now!"

I quickly bend over and grasp the edge of the granite countertop. I feel the tip of his cock moving back and forth in my wetness, and then without warning, he slams in so deep I can feel it in my stomach. "Oh my God!"

"Feel that, angel. I'm so deep inside you I can feel your fucking womb."

"Oh shit," I gasp, "I feel it." And I love it. David has stamina and strength. He thrusts into me so hard and so long I nearly pass out by the time he finally comes. I almost come again but not quite. It's okay. It isn't important. Sex has never felt that good before.

"You didn't come," he mutters, still inside me. He reaches around and uses his hand to circle and squeeze my clit. In seconds, I'm coming so hard that I'm squeezing him inside of me. When I moan, he moans. "Perfect," he says, tiredly kissing the back of my neck. "Fucking perfect."

When he slides out of me, I feel wetness drip down the inside my legs. We didn't use a condom. Am I sad about that? Not really. I know he's been tested. I made him the appointment after he kicked his wife out. I opened the letter with the results myself since they sent them to the office. I used to open *all* his mail. He says nothing. He grabs me by the hand and pulls me out of the kitchen. "Bedroom."

I point to the stairs leading up. Once in my bedroom, he leads me to my en suite bathroom. He lets go of my hand to turn on my steam shower. With the temperature just right, he opens the door and steps inside, waving me to come into the shower with him. "Uh, what are we doing?" I've never showered with a man.

"You're a dirty girl, Cass. Time to clean you up," he quips.

I say nothing. What *can* I say? I step into my own shower and let him wash me from head to toe. I've never had a more thorough or sensual shower.

I return the favor, but as I'm about to clean his hard cock, he grabs my wrist to stop me. "On your knees, angel."

My God, he's so alpha. I knew he was bossy, but I never imagined. Why is that so hot? I hold on to the bar in the shower and lower myself to my knees. It doesn't hurt, but it's not super comfortable either.

I look up at him and see a smile appear on his face. "Open," he growls.

I nearly come from that alone. I open my mouth and let him slide the head inside. I can taste him, salty and musky. I suck him, licking the tip at the same time. He moans so loud it echoes around my bathroom. "Good, honey. Do that again."

So, I do it again. I suck and lick and nibble. He seems to like the nibbles right under the crown of his dick the best. He slides both hands into my hair, and I know what's coming—no pun intended. He holds my head still as he slowly thrusts in and out, shallow at first. Then his thrusts gradually getting deeper. There's no way I can take all of him, but he tries. When he hits the back of my throat, I grasp his wrist. He pulls out of my mouth and leans down to help me up. "You okay?" he asks gently. I nod. He gives me a sweet, gentle kiss. "That was unbelievable, Cassie. The best."

I look down at him and see he's still rigid. Using my hand, I slide my palm over his shaft and begin to move it up and down.

"Yeah, Cass, yeah," he says. His voice husky. "Finish me off."

I don't have to work long when he comes hard and fast.

"So, good," he says, taking in deep breaths.

I turn and rinse my hand as I smile back at him, then turn off the water. I doubt it was that good. He's been with some seriously gorgeous women who've probably obtained master's degrees in oral sex. That was the first time I've ever done that. It couldn't have been that great.

Stepping out of my shower, I find David is already holding up a towel for me. I walk into it, and he wraps it around my body. He dries my shoulders and arms then moves down to my waist and hips. He runs the towel into my center and then up to my breasts. He takes extra care there, so much so I start to giggle, making everything on my body jiggle and shake.

"What's so funny?" he asks, looking hurt.

I giggle again. "You're spending a lot of time on the girls," I say, pointing to my breasts.

When he realizes that he was, in fact, focused on my breasts, he laughs. "I can't help it. They're very, very special."

I throw my head back and laugh for real. "I had no idea," I say, gasping for air.

"Well, now you do. Let's get in bed, and I'll tell you more about it."

What? He wants to get in my bed? I should say no. I should stop this right now, but I know what this is, and it's not long-term. I don't mind. I'll let him in my bed. This girl has needs too.

17

DAVID

JUST BECAUSE IT'S A BAD IDEA DOESN'T MEAN IT WON'T BE A GOOD TIME.

What the fuck am I doing? Oh, I remember, I'm fucking my assistant so hard my balls want to call a truce. I've had her four times in the last five hours—on her counter, in her shower, in her bed, and on her white couch in her feminine sitting room. She's going to have to get that thing cleaned because we both came like a nuclear bomb. She was on top straddling me. Her hands were on the back of the sofa while mine were on her amazing hips. From that vantage point, I got to watch her tits bounce. Jesus, I don't remember sex feeling that good, *ever*.

So, that means I'm fucked. This can't continue. It's a one-night thing. I'm pretty sure she understands that—not that we talked about it. We haven't talked much, to be honest, unless you're referring to dirty talk. She got pretty good at it by the end of our last session. So good, I think I've created a monster. Right now, we're back in her bed. She's wrapped around me like a warm blanket. My hand is on her ass, and I'm running my palm back and forth. Her skin is so soft. She's not wearing a bunch of stinky lotions and makeup, so I get to smell pure woman. Pure fucked woman. That's the best kind.

Damn, the woman can take my cock like no one else. Jennifer was too frail to take it the way I like it. I would have snapped her in half like a twig if I pummeled her like I just did Cass. I've missed that kind of sex. The kind that's passionate and powerful—the kind that takes the wind out of you. "Damn," I say as I reposition my body. "The kind that makes your muscles hurt." I chuckle. It was a rigorous workout.

I peer down at her. She's got curves everywhere. Her belly is a little too round and full. Her thighs may be a little bit too big, and I see dimples on those as well. I run my fingers over one or two spots and don't feel disgusted by them. Her arms aren't firm or toned like Jennifer's, but Jen's were more like leather over bone. Cassie's are soft and fleshy. They feel good wrapped around me.

I move her hair away from her beautiful face, and I spot that beauty mark. Just seeing it makes me hard again. I lean down and swipe my tongue over the tiny dot. She moves like she's waking up, and my dick hardens further. I wonder if she can take me again. I lean down and kiss her on the corner of her mouth as one eye flutters open. "Again?" she says in a husky morning voice.

"Again." I pull the blanket away from us, pushing it onto the floor. I want to see her entire body as I fuck her from behind again. "Hands on the headboard, Cassie." She rolls over to her stomach and pushes her ass up first. Using her hands, she climbs up until she grasps the top edge of her headboard. She looks back at me with a sleepy smile. Damn, she's amazing. "Push that big ass out, honey."

I see her stiffen immediately. Her back is rigid, and she's no longer looking at me. Her face is straight ahead. Without looking at me, she says, "Uh, I'm a little sore, David."

"You don't have to do a thing. I'll do all the work, honey," I reply as I slide my palm over her bottom.

She pulls away from the front of the bed and sits back on her heels. Grabbing the sheet next to her side of the bed, she wraps it around herself and slides out of bed. "I'm too sore. Sorry." She walks into the bathroom and shuts the door.

I hear the lock, and I blink at the door. "What just happened?"

When she reappears, she's wearing a T-shirt and shorts. Her closet must be in there. Confused, I ask, "So, we're done?"

She gives me a smile, but it doesn't reach those gorgeous green eyes. "Yep. We're done." She walks out of her bedroom door, and I listen as her footsteps move down the steps.

Why do I get the feeling her statement had double meaning? I jump out of bed in search of my clothes. I remember tossing them down onto the kitchen floor, so I walk downstairs naked. She's in the kitchen making coffee when I spot my clothes folded neatly on the kitchen counter. I want to say something, but I'm not sure what that should be. So, I go with, "Are we okay?"

She turns, giving me that fake-ass smile again. "Of course. Would you like some coffee in a travel cup?"

"I'm leaving?" I guess I'm leaving. I pull on my sweats and tee.

"You've got work today, right? I've got to get going on my resumes." She hands me a Chicago Bears travel mug, one that I gave her for Christmas a few years back. It looks brand new. Maybe she doesn't like the Bears as much as I do.

"I'll get this back to you," I say, pointing to the cup.

"Don't bother. I never use that one."

"Oh, okay." I look around the floor for my shoes and see them in her hand. I take them and slip them on. I look up and see she's made her way to the door. This is getting old. She doesn't need to escort me to the fucking door. "Jesus," I mutter.

I stomp down her steps and yank the door open. I look over

at her and see her eyes are shiny. Is she going to fucking cry? "Are you going to fucking cry?"

She pulls her shoulders back and lifts her head proudly. "No. Of course not. Goodbye, David."

"Is this because I said you had a big ass?"

I watch her wince at the words.

"Well, I've got news for you, honey. You've got big everything." She does. She's voluptuous and the goddamn sexiest woman I've ever met. It's not a fucking secret. Jesus. I run my fingers through my hair. I can't deal with this low self-esteem bullshit. "Goodbye! Have a good life!" I say loudly. And good riddance. What the fuck did I do wrong? Women! They're all the same!

I slam the door as soon as I'm on her front step. I hear her engage the locks, and I'm out of there. I stomp down the street to my car. I hit my key fob, slide inside, slam the door shut, and squeal out of my parking spot on the street. "Fucking women!"

18

CASSANDRA

THEY'LL HATE YOU IF YOU'RE PRETTY, THEY'LL HATE YOU IF YOU'RE NOT. THEY'LL HATE YOU FOR WHAT YOU LACK, AND THEY'LL HATE YOU FOR WHAT YOU'VE GOT.

I was overly sensitive when he told me to "push that big ass out," but I can't help it. When it comes to comments about my size, a whole slew of bad memories rush back to me. Every time a guy told me I was fat or ugly or gross crawls back into my psyche like a spider in a web. In my heart, I know he didn't mean it that way, but I can't help how I reacted. I'm just glad I waited until the door slammed behind him for the tears to fall.

I slowly walk back up to the kitchen to grab my cup of coffee and my box of tissues when I hear pounding on my door. "Shit!" I growl. Apparently, he's not finished saying what he needs to say. I stomp back down the steps, unlock the door, and yank it open. I'm about to say something rude when I see who it is. It's not David, but I wish it was because instead of David, it's Jennifer Flynn. At six in the morning, she looks like she's ready to go to a garden party in her tight, sleeveless, floral sheath dress, five-inch stilettos, perfectly coifed hair, makeup and nails, and an expression that screams mean girl. "Jen?"

"Well, hello Mama Cass." She pushes past me into the condo uninvited. Her heels click and clack as she stomps up the steps.

I do not need this right now. "Can I help you, Jennifer? How did you find out where I lived?"

"David told me." She looks around my home then stares daggers at me. "Did David buy you this place?"

"No!" I'm going to kill David. I walk to my kitchen and around the counter, so something separates us. She makes me nervous. Her expression screams rabid animal. "What do you want, Jen?"

She sets her five-hundred-dollar Michael Kors bag down on the counter and follows me around to stand directly in front of me. My first inclination is to keep moving, but I decide to stand my ground. "I came to find out how long my husband has been fucking his fat-ass assistant. By the looks of this place, I'd say it's been a good long while."

"Excuse me?"

"You heard me, *piglet*. How long have you and Dave been fucking?"

"We haven't—" I don't get the rest out when she interrupts.

"I just watched him leave your place. Unless you were working on some big investment deal... oh wait, you don't work for him anymore. So, why was he here All. Night. Long?"

She was watching my house all night? "It's none of your business. I want you to leave."

She steps toward me, and I back up further until I'm cornered. The only way out is behind Jennifer. "You listen to me, fatso. I will not sit back and let my husband fall victim to a whale like you. His idiot brothers are too far gone to listen, so it's up to *me* to help him preserve his reputation. He can't be seen with the likes of *you*," she says, poking my chest with her red claw-like fingernail. "He's my husband and—"

"You're divorced." I spit.

"Do *not* interrupt me," she shouts. She presses me back until the counter is digging into my lower back.

It hurts, so much so I attempt to push back, but the tiny bitch is stronger than she looks. "Back off, Jen."

"Or what?"

Or what? "Just back off. There's nothing going on."

She pushes me so hard my head slams back into the wall. Screaming, she shouts, "I watched him leave your place at five thirty in the fucking morning!"

I make one more attempt to push her off me. Luckily, I catch her off balance, and I'm able to rush past her out of the kitchen. When I turn around, pain shoots through my eye and nose. I fall to my knees from the shock of the blow. I lift my hand to my face and feel wetness. Blood. I look up and see a crazy Jennifer Flynn, her eyes bulging out of her head and her fists clenched like she's going to take another swing at me.

I swing my leg out and around, catching her ankles as it goes around. I hear her yelp and see her knees buckle then watch her fall to the ground. I crawl over to her and grab her hands, so she can't hit me. I straddle her scrawny hips. "Don't you ever hit me again, you bitch! Don't you ever come to my home again, or I will end you. Do you hear me?" I spit the words out and watch the blood drip off of my face onto her pretty dress.

"You're ruining my dress," she screeches.

I lift my body up with my legs then slam myself back on top of her. She grunts from the force. "I said, do you hear me?"

"God, yes. Get off me. You're suffocating me."

"Good." I release her hands and throw my leg over and off of her. As I'm pulling myself upward, I feel her claws dig into my face. "Jesus, why?" I scream, bringing my hand up to my cheek. "Why do you have to be like this? I did nothing to you."

"You fucked my husband," she growls.

"You. Are. Divorced."

She screams like a psycho banshee and runs at me like she actually wants to kill me. I back away right before she can make contact. It also happens to be right at the top of the stairs. She loses her balance and falls down the three tiled steps to the entryway. God, I hope she broke something—an arm, a fingernail, anything.

I reach for my phone and dial the cops. "911. What is your emergency?"

"I was attacked in my own home. She's still here. Send someone fast." I list my address and hear her moan.

"You fucking fat cunt," she growls. She pulls herself up to her knees. One of her fancy shoes is on the stairs, the other is on her foot, but the heel is broken.

"And you're a psycho. No amount of dieting is gonna cure that," I spit back.

She lets out a blood-curdling scream as she charges back up the steps. She's limping but still fast for someone who is obviously injured. I step backward, attempting to get away from her, but I'm not fast enough. She launches her body into the air, wrapping her fingers around my neck. We fall to the ground with me on the bottom and her on top this time. Her claws are digging into my neck, and her legs are wrapped tightly around my waist. Why didn't I run into the bathroom and lock the door? I'm such an idiot. If I get out of this alive, I'm taking some damned self-defense classes.

She's got such a tight grip around my neck that it's hard to breathe. How did I let this happen? I'm stronger than this. This is all David's fault. I swear I'm going to kill him. It's a shame I love the asshole so much. If I didn't, I'd believe my own threats. I gasp for air as things around me start to get foggy. I hear pounding and voices shouting off in the distance then a loud crashing sound. More voices surround me. Shots. Gunshots? It's the last thing on my mind as everything fades to black.

19

DAVID

A GOOD WOMAN WILL BE A MAN'S PEACE AND A
GOOD MAN WILL BE A WOMAN'S PROTECTION.

I'm scowling when I get to work. When Gretchen sees me, she shows the common sense to stay away from me this morning, thank fuck. I stomp into my office and slam the door behind me. I rip my jacket off and throw it on the couch. I get to my fucking ergonomic chair, and all I want to do is throw it through my fucking floor-to-ceiling windows.

But, of course, I don't do that. I do, however, toss the fucker into the middle of my office. I drag one of the chairs from in front of my desk to use instead. It's too large to fit under my desk, but I don't care. I toss my feet up on my desk and grab my tablet and set it in my lap. Logging into my email, I see several from Lester about a meeting this morning. "Jesus, I'm in no mood for a fucking meeting." All I want to do is think about something other than Cassie. Something other than the most amazing sex I've ever had—the most amazing night of my life. I need something to take my mind off of her—anything to divert my thoughts. When my cell rings, part of me hopes it's her. Maybe she's calling to apologize for kicking me out, for treating me like garbage. I pick it up and see Hank's name on the screen. "Great." I hit the green circle. "What?"

"You need to get to Rush River North."

"What? Why? What's wrong?"

"It's Cassie. She's been attacked."

"Attacked? By who? When?"

"Jesus, bro. Get here. I'm in the ER." I hear the phone click off, and I'm out of my seat so fast the tablet tumbles to the floor. I jump over it and race to the door, grabbing my jacket on the way. I throw open my door and shout at Gretchen as I pass. "Emergency. Need to get to the hospital."

"But... but you've got a meeting with Uncle, er, Mr. Ingot."

"Reschedule."

"He'll be mad," she says challengingly, hands on her hips.

"I don't give a fuck. I said it's an *emergency!*" I take off at a run to get to the elevator. If it takes too long, I'll take the stairs. But the gods must be listening because it chimes open as I approach. I shove a guy out of my way and start hitting the L button for the lobby. I pull my phone out and call Hank. When his voice mail picks up, I say, "Call me. Tell me what's going on. Is she okay? Who attacked her?" I hang up and watch the numbers on the elevator as they descend. It takes forever. Once the doors open on the street level, I run out to the sidewalk to grab the first available cab. A bright yellow sedan stops, and I throw myself in the seat. "Rush River North Emergency. Fast!"

The taxi driver squeals out of the spot and guns it. The hospital is close, but the traffic is heavy at this time of morning. That doesn't seem to faze this driver because I'm there in less than ten minutes. I toss a hundred-dollar bill at him and run in through the glass doors. Hank is nowhere to be found, so I text him.

Me: I'm here. In the waiting room. Get out here.

Hank: Be out in a few minutes.

I sit down, but I can't sit still. I jump up and start to pace. But that, apparently, annoys an older woman, so I sit back down. The cycle begins again. "Jesus, where are you, Hank?" I say out loud.

"Here. I'm right here, Dave."

I see my big brother exiting a security door. I get up and meet him halfway. "What's going on? What happened?"

Hank taps my arm and points to an alcove in the back of the waiting area. A minute later, in relative privacy, Hank looks at me and shakes his head. "There were two 9-1-1 calls. One from Cassie and another from a neighbor after hearing screams. When the officers got there, she was unconscious and severely beaten."

"Who the hell beat her up?"

Hank rolls his head back and forth on his neck, like he's trying to release some tension. He takes a deep breath. "Jen. It was Jennifer."

"Jennifer who?"

With one brow arched, Hank deadpans, "Jennifer Flynn, dumbass."

"My ex? Why? Why would she attack Cassie? Cassie's only ever been nice to her." I shake the thoughts from my head. "Why?" I ask again.

"You tell me. Why would Jennifer feel the need to attack Cassie? How did she even know where Cassie lives?"

I blink at my brother because I know the answer to both of those questions. "She must've followed me there last night. That's how she knew."

"Last night?" asks Hank. "Why would she wait until this morning to knock on Cassie's door?"

I blink a few times before I respond. When I tell Hank that I spent the night at Cassie's place, he's going to want the entire story. "I spent the night at, um, Cassandra's."

"You stayed the night with Cassie?" Hank rolls his eyes. "Jesus, you're fucking with her head, man. If you don't love her—"

I ignore his forthcoming lecture. "How is she? Where is she?"

"Who? Jen?"

"No. Cassie. Is she okay?"

Hank sighs. "I haven't seen her yet, but the ER doc says she's beat to hell. Broken nose, deep-ass scratches on her face, bruising on her neck."

"Bruises on her neck?"

"Yeah, the cops got there in the nick of time. Jennifer was on top of her. Strangling her."

"You're fucking with me." That can't be possible. "And Jen?"

"Cops shot her."

"What?" I shouted.

"Shoulder wound. A through and through. Missed anything vital. They treated her and released her into police custody. Wish they'd have put her down for good, but"—he shrugs—"we can't have everything we want."

I nod. I agree with him, but don't say it out loud. "Where is she now?"

Hank glares at me. He looks at his watch and sighs. "Your psycho ex-wife should be getting booked for assault with intent right about now." Hank looks up at the ceiling then back to me. "Cassie needs to get a restraining order against that bitch as soon as possible."

"She will. I'll make sure of it. Can you get me back there to see Cassie?"

"I'll try." Hank stands and walks back to the ER. All he has to do is flash his badge, and they let him pass.

I only have to wait a few minutes for Hank to come back.

He glares at me like I'm lower than a deadly bacterium. "What the hell did you do to her?"

"What do you mean?"

"She doesn't want to see you."

"What? Why not?"

"You tell me. What did you do to piss her off?"

I lay my head back and sigh. "I may have told her this morning that she has a big ass."

"Jesus, dude. You're a fucking tool."

"I know! I didn't mean it the way it sounded. What do I need to do to get back there?"

"Well, when Sophie was brought in, I told them she was my fiancée. Worked like a charm."

"Sounds good to me." I stand up and march over to the admissions desk. "My fiancée was brought in this morning. Cassandra Darrow. I need to see her."

A few minutes later, I'm buzzed back into the emergency ward and I search for room 6B. When I find the room, I open the curtain and stop dead in my tracks. My heart pounds out of my chest, and my stomach drops. Cassie looks like she was run over by a truck. I suddenly feel nauseous. "Cassie?" I choke. An overwhelming sense of worry hits me. Now, *I* feel like I've been hit by a truck. Doing my best to keep the emotions out of my voice, I whisper. "Baby?" A tear slides down my cheek as I walk over to her. She's asleep. She's got a tube in her nose and an IV in her arm. She's hooked up to a machine that beeps continuously. I feel horrible. Guilty. "I'm responsible for this," I whisper. "This is my fault, honey. I'm so sorry."

"You should be." Her voice is weak. "That wicked witch of an ex-wife almost killed me."

I can't help it; I chuckle through the tears running down my face. Her one good eye squints at me, and it's not a happy look. "You told her where I lived?"

"No. I think she followed me last night."

"Makes sense. She knows you stayed all night." She winces in pain when she tries to move a little bit. "Everything hurts. God, I hate you so much right now."

It's my turn to wince. "I'm sorry. I'm really sorry, honey."

She lets out a breath. Even breathing looks painful for her. "I know. It's not your fault. It's just the pain talking. She's crazy—scary crazy, David. She needs to be in a mental hospital."

I chuckle.

She turns that one good eye on me again. "I'm completely and utterly serious. She's clinically insane."

"She's just jealous."

"If you think she did this to me out of jealousy, you're even more stupid than I thought. She's...." Cassie hesitates. "Trust me. She needs help."

"We'll get a restraining order against her."

She attempts to scoff, but it comes out weak. "That will *not* stop her, David."

"I'll protect you." And I will. It's time I step up and do right by Cassandra. She deserves my full attention. Did I just hear her scoff again? "You don't think I can keep you safe?"

"No. I'm sure in that macho, alpha mind of yours you think you can, but you can't be with me 24/7. It's just not feasible."

"Yes, I can," I say a little defensively. I'll just have to prove it to her.

20

CASSANDRA

KEEP CALM & FIND YOUR HAPPY PLACE.

I spent the night in the hospital. The doctor in charge of my case wanted to make sure I was breathing and swallowing without pain before he'd release me. While I hated the hospital bed, I didn't mind staying because I felt safe. I can't explain it—I'm not used to fear. I grew up on a dairy farm in a little town in Iowa. Nothing bad happened to people there unless you count the time my mom ran off with the milkman—no joke. She ran off with a dairy sales rep for our county. I haven't seen her in sixteen years.

Right now, I feel uneasy about being alone in my home. I know Jennifer is in police custody. Hank Flynn told me she'll remain in jail for the time being. I also know that I need to press charges to prevent her from getting out anytime soon. My attorney will need to file a restraining order against her. She's a very unstable person. David doesn't believe me. He thinks she's just jealous. That, my friends, was not jealousy. That was a textbook example of *cray-cray*.

I'm lost in thought when my nurse, Nancy, steps in my room. "Time to get you ready, honey. Doctor Mann said you're good to go."

"Oh, okay. Great."

She looks over at me and smiles. "You okay, sweetie? Do you need anything?"

I sigh. "Just courage. I don't want to go back to my place yet."

"Well, I overheard your young man tell Dr. Mann that you're going home with him. That's why Dr. Mann is letting you go so soon."

"What young man?"

"Mr. Flynn."

I growl, and it hurts. "He's *not* my young man. He's the reason I'm in this position."

Nancy looks shocked. "*He* did this to you?" she says, pointing at my face. "Why didn't you tell us? I'll call the police."

"No! No, that's not what I meant. His ex-wife did this to me. David had no idea." So, I should stop blaming him.

"Oh, phew, I thought I was gonna have to whoop his ass." She chuckles.

I smile. "I'll take care of that. He's not out of the woods just yet."

"Who's not out of the woods just yet?" asks the man in question.

"Your ears must be burnin'," Nancy cackles.

"You're talking about me?" He smiles smugly. "Doc says you can come home now."

"David—"

"Now, I know what you're going to say, Cass. I'm sure you don't feel comfortable going back to your place yet. Am I right?"

I nod.

"And my place is secure. No one will be able to get on the elevator without the doorman authorizing it."

I stare at him. I know he's right. I'm just uncomfortable going to his place.

"So, it's settled. You're moving in with me."

"Moving in?" I squeak. "I don't—"

"Just until you're back on your feet. I've got a spare bedroom. You'll be very comfortable. I'll be able to keep you safe that way."

I put on a fake smile and nod again. *The spare bedroom?* I've been relegated to the spare bedroom. I need to find my happy place because my life has taken a downward spiral, and it seems to keep right on spinning. Sadly, I'm in no position to stop it.

21

DAVID

LOVE ISN'T ABOUT FINDING THE PERFECT PERSON;
IT'S ABOUT REALIZING THAT AN IMPERFECT PERSON
CAN MAKE YOUR LIFE PERFECT.

Having Cassandra in my home is strange. But good. Very good. I like coming home from work and finding her curled up on my couch reading a book. I like all of her girly shit strewn across the bathroom counter. I like her scent all around my place. I don't know if it's her soap or what, but she's everywhere. I pull my keys out of my pocket to unlock the door. When I open it, the first thing I notice is the smell. It's not her subtle flowery scent. No, this time it smells like she's cooking, and it smells fucking delicious. Coming home from a hard day at work to find my woman has cooked for me? My dick just got hard.

I set my briefcase down near the door and walk through the living room into my kitchen. I stop in the doorway to see Cassie bent over looking inside the oven. It's the most beautiful sight I've ever seen, no joke. I groan loudly at the sight of her luscious ass. I hear the squeak and watch her stand up so fast she gets a little off balance. I rush over to her and place my hands on her arms. "You okay?"

She giggles. That giggle is a sound that I don't think I will ever get tired of. "You startled me," she says, slapping my chest.

"Sorry." I lean in and kiss her nose. "You're cooking? You must be feeling better." She's been here just over a week. The first few days were touch and go. No, she wasn't about to die. What I mean is that I wasn't sure who wanted to kill who the most. Cassie or me. Getting used to having a roommate again has been an adjustment. It's not like Jennifer had much of a presence in our place. She didn't cook because she didn't eat. She didn't clean or read or have meaningful conversations with me. She spent her time at home either talking on her phone or texting her friends—and lovers. Most of Jen's time was spent shopping or at some salon or spa. We slept together, sure. We had sex, of course. It wasn't good sex. Jen loved being in control. I've since realized that sex with her was unfulfilling; one night with Cassie has shown me that. I just went through the motions with Jennifer, so I could come and so she'd get off of me. Jesus. Why did I stay with her?

I'm pulled from my thoughts when Cassie says, "I am feeling better. I'm no longer taking the pain meds, so I've got some energy today."

"What're you making? It smells delicious."

"Nothing fancy. I just made a vegetable lasagna."

I grinned. "I love lasagna."

"Well, you're going to have to share. Your parents are coming to dinner."

Jesus, I feel like I'm in an episode of the *Dick Van Dyke Show*. "When did that all happen?"

"This morning. Your mom called to check on me, and one thing led to another."

"Okay. Let me go change. Then I'll come in and help you."

Cassie smiles sweetly at me, and my focus moves to her beauty mark. It's been over a week since I had a taste, so I lean in and gently wrap my arms around her. I pull her closer and look into her eyes. "I'm glad you're feeling better, baby." I lean down and kiss the beauty mark. My mouth moves down to her soft lips, and I kiss her gently there too. She's still got bruising and cuts on her face, so I know she's sore. When she opens her mouth and swipes my lips with hers, I moan. I pull her closer to me, turn my head slightly, and go for it. My tongue moves in and touches hers. I bring one hand up and slide it into her knotted hair. My dick is granite. I press it into her stomach, so she knows how turned on I am.

"When will my parents be here?"

"Thirty minutes," she rasps.

"I need you, Cass. I need to sink into you right now. Are you up for it?"

She nods. I grab her hand and lead her to my bedroom, the place I've wanted her since she moved in, but I didn't want to roll over and hurt her in my sleep. Sleeping in the spare room was for the best—for her. Even though it sucked. I rush to the bedroom, pulling her along with me. When we get to my room, I turn and rip her top right off her body. I reach around and release the most gorgeous tits I've ever seen. Leaning down, I press my face between them and lick. She tastes sweet and salty. I latch on to a nipple and look up. Cassie's head is thrown back, and her palm is on the back of my head now. I place my fingers into the waistband of her yoga pant things and slide them down her legs. I step back to look at her. She's no longer bare. Some of her natural hair has grown back now, and I love it. Pulling her by the hand, I back her up until she's sitting on my bed. "Lay back, honey. Spread your legs. Let me look."

She lets out a soft moan and does exactly as I ask. Goddamn, I love how submissive she is. My dick grows even harder, which doesn't seem possible. Her pink folds are wet and glistening for me. I slide my fingers through, and when I get to her hard, little clit, I use my thumb and first finger to rub circles around it. I pinch it a few times, and she wriggles in the bed. "Touch your tits, Cass. Pull on your nipples."

She does as I say. "Jesus, you look hot as sin doing that. I need to be inside you."

"Yes," she hisses. "Do it. Fuck me, David." She's so ready for me she's sliding her ass closer to me.

I grab onto her hips and move between her thick thighs. It's such a sweet feeling being between her legs. It's warm, and it feels like home. When I slowly slide my cock into her tight opening, we both groan loudly. "I've missed you so much, Cass," I mutter.

"Me too," she whimpers. "Harder, David."

This time, I'll let her tell me what to do. I pull out and thrust in so hard I push her to the middle of the bed. When I pull out, she whines, "What are you doing? No."

"Up on your hands and knees, babe."

She does as I ask, and I pull her until her knees are on the edge of the bed. I place one knee on the bed beside her leg, and now I'm in the perfect position. I slide my dick back in slowly. The tension surrounding my dick is hard to explain. She's tight and warm. So fucking warm.

"Oh shit, David. Do it again. It feels so good this way."

"I know. I'm gonna come so deep inside you, baby. I'm gonna put my kid in there." Ironically, I always wore a rubber when I was with Jennifer, and I haven't worn one at all with Cassie. I'm not sure why. Jennifer was even on the pill. Maybe I should have given that some thought before I married her.

We both stop moving. She slowly turns her head. Her beautiful emerald eyes tell me everything I want to know. She wants that too. We say nothing to each other as I slam back in, harder this time. I'm gonna knock her the fuck up. I can't wait until she's round with my kid. "Mine, Cassie. You're mine. You got that?"

"Yes. All yours. Harder, David."

I lean forward and hold her tits, lifting her body up until her back is pressing against my front. I thrust up so hard I feel her jiggle. It's perfect. Fucking perfect. "So good." I reach down and find her clit again. I use pressure to rub around it and over it back and forth until I feel her come before she even moans. She's coming so hard, squeezing my dick until I think I'm going to black out.

I shout as my come shoots deep inside her. I hold still and let it pump out of me. When I finally pull away, I watch my cum slide out of her. I place my hand between her legs to hold it inside. "Lay down on your back." She does as I ask. I grab a pillow. "Lift your hips." I slide the pillow under her ass to elevate it. "That'll keep my boys in there longer." She blinks up at me, and I see her eyes glistening. "I mean it, Cassie. I love you, honey. I want this. Please tell me you do too." She nods as the first tear slides down her cheek. In ten years, I've rarely seen her cry. "I hope to fuck those are happy tears." She nods again. I lean down and kiss the one that just ran over her beauty mark. I swipe my tongue over it and taste her salty tears. "You okay? That may have been too much for you so soon after...."

"I'm good." She smiles sweetly.

"You are good. You're the best I've ever had, Cassie. And I'm not just talking about sex. You're the best everything." She lets out a sob now, and I watch as more tears fall down her plump cheeks. I run into the bathroom and grab some tissue. "Shh, it's going to be okay. I've got you." I wrap my arms around her and pull her into my chest. "I've got you."

22

CASSANDRA

LOVE IS A WORD USED TOO MUCH AND MUCH TOO SOON.

Minutes after David and I snuggle up together, his doorbell rings. "Shit!" he exclaims jumping out of bed. "You okay?" he says, pulling on his dress shirt then his slacks.

"Going commando?"

"No time to grab clean boxers," he says, placing a finger over his lips. "Shh, our secret." He chuckles, looking for some socks. "Get dressed. I'll get them a drink, so take your time." I sit up in bed. "Uh, you'd better brush your hair or something. You definitely look like you've been fucked into next week."

I groan. "Thanks."

"Oh, you're very welcome," he says, beaming at me. "It was all my pleasure." He winks as he leaves his bedroom.

I slide out of bed, wincing. He did screw me into next week. My body hurts. I bend down to pick up my clothes and step into the bathroom. In his mirror, I wince. "Oh, crap." I look like something the cat dragged in. I dress quickly, brush out my hair, and use a warm washcloth on my face. I stop by my bedroom to grab a hair tie and work it up into a bun. "This is as good as it's gonna get." When I make it to the kitchen, I see Sarah and

Declan Flynn sitting on David's barstools. They turn when they hear me. "Well, hello, honey. How are you feeling?" asks Sarah.

I smile because Sarah Flynn is a wonderful person. She's sweet and sincere, and she loves her family with every fiber of her being. "I'm good. Feeling much better."

"You look better," mumbles Declan.

I chuckle. "It'll take a bit more time but I'll heal."

"I still can't believe she did it," mutters Declan again. "Crazy bitch."

I let out a shocked laugh. I don't ever remember hearing him cuss. "She is," I agree.

"Come on. She's not crazy," admonishes David. "She's just jealous."

"You're kidding, right?" snaps Sarah. "She's a nutjob."

"Mom! Stop. She is not."

"You're defending her?" Sarah asks, standing.

"I'm not. She's just not insane or crazy. She's misunderstood."

"You're fucking kidding me," Sarah squeaks, red-faced.

It is important to note that Sarah never, and I mean never, uses bad words. She's diametrically opposed to profanity. So, if she uses the f-word, it's fucking serious.

David gasps. "Mom? You said the f-word."

"I know! And if you say one more word in defense of that woman, I'm leaving."

"Mom?"

"Honey?" adds Declan.

"No! I'm serious!" she says with her hands on her tiny hips.

"Fine, Mom. Not another word," David mutters.

I clear my throat and turn toward the kitchen. "Need to check the lasagna." I had left it on warm in the oven. I hope it's not dried out thanks to our little tryst. I grab an oven mitt and open the door, sending the scent of Italian spices and tomato sauce billowing up into the air.

Both Flynn men moan. "That smells amazing," says Declan. David nods in agreement.

"There's salad in the fridge, David. Can you grab it?"

I have a pan of garlic bread ready to go in, so I bring out the lasagna and slide in the bread. "Once the bread is done, we're ready to eat. Shall we use your dining table, David?" He's used to eating on his sofa. He's even got a set of TV trays against one wall.

"Sure. What does everyone want to drink?"

"Water," says Sarah.

"Beer," responds Declan.

"Water for me, please," I say, smiling at David. When he smiles back, a chill runs up my spine. This whole thing is so domestic. It's like we're a married couple hosting a small dinner party. I quickly look away from him, pretending to check on the bread I put in the oven seconds before. It's overwhelming—the idea that David Flynn loves me. It's surreal.

I hand David the pan of lasagna and a trivet to set on the table. I search the drawers for a serving spatula and tongs for the salad. I find everything just where it should be. Handing him the tools, I peek at the bread and see it's toasted perfectly. I grab the pan and set each piece of toasted bread in a basket. Walking out to the table, I find all three Flynns are smiling widely at me.

"This is lovely," says Sarah, beaming. "I could get used to coming over here for dinner."

I look at David, who smiles at me. "Me too." He winks.

I sit down and hand Declan the basket of bread. We pass the dishes around, and as soon as we're ready to eat, Declan asks, "So, what's going on with Beranger Aeronautics?"

"Oh, yeah. I'd forgotten all about that. How'd their IPO go?"

"What's IPO?" asks Sarah.

I turn to her. "It stands for Initial Public Offering. Also known as a stock market launch in which shares of a company usually are sold to institutional investors that, in turn, sell to the general public on a securities exchange for the first time. The IPO process is colloquially known as going public."

I look up at see everyone staring at me. "What?"

"Shit, Cass. I knew you were well versed in the business, but I had no idea you could recite, verbatim, the definition of IPO?" David chuckles.

I shrug. "There's a lot you don't know about me," I add smugly, taking a small bite of salad.

"Oh yeah? Like what?" he asks, challenging me.

I shrug, choosing to ignore his question and ask one instead. "So, what did happen with Beranger?"

"They had a great first-day pop. Their prices have been rising fast."

I nod. "Has anything new come out about their space technology?"

"Nothing new. They've just been sending out teasers to keep the stocks up. They put out a YouTube simulation animation that got things moving on day one."

"Smart," I mutter. "Dr. Brown was always smart." Add to that rude and creepy. "Anything else happening with Lester?"

"Not that I can tell. He hasn't been back in my office again. I have caught Gretchen on camera touching me, sitting on my desk, leaning over way too far. She even tried to rub my shoulders as she whispered in my ear about an upcoming meeting." I watch him shiver. "She's a creep."

"Okay, this is all news to me," says Sarah. "Who is Gretchen and why is she touching you without your permission?"

I nearly spit out my bite of salad as I giggle. That was funny.

"Mom," David whines, "it's just my assistant. She's very

touchy-feely. I don't like it, and I worry she'll turn the tables on me. That's why Hank set up cameras and audio equipment in my office."

Sarah nods. "Smart thinking. You can't trust anyone anymore." She turns to me. "Except you, sweetie. You were always trustworthy. It's a shame you quit."

I look up at David and see him avoiding my gaze. He didn't tell her everything. "Uh, yeah, well, I had other things in the works."

"Like what?" David asks sternly. "What else don't I know about you?"

I sigh. "Well, I've got my MBA from Loyola."

He blinks at me. "When did you get that?" He sounds pissed.

"Five years ago."

"Mm-hm, what else?" he asks suspiciously.

"Well, I've passed every FINRA and NFA investment licensing exam. And—"

He scoffs. "Impossible. Every one of them?"

I nod. "It took me a long time, but I just finished up last week."

"That had to cost a fortune. I know those tests are expensive," Sarah says, interrupting and breaking some of the tension.

"I've made a lot of money investing." I look up at David, who's scowling at me now.

"With whom? Who have you invested with? Because it wasn't me."

"I'm licensed in the state of Illinois. But in answer to how I've made money, a few of my former classmates from Loyola and I started an Investment Club as soon as we graduated. We've been very successful."

"Jesus," he mutters, standing up from the table and taking his plate into the kitchen.

I smile over at Sarah, who's beaming at me. She leans over and pats my hand. "Good for you, Cassandra. Good for you. A woman needs to be able to take care of herself before she can take care of the people she loves."

I nod, not really understanding what she's talking about. My mom took care of herself—but only herself.

Declan nods with his mouth full of lasagna. Winking, he says, "She's right. Don't let my chauvinistic son get to you."

That comment makes me giggle. David *can* be a chauvinist. He can't seem to help himself. Maybe I can teach him a new way of thinking. "Well, if he thinks I'm going to stay home barefoot and pregnant—"

I look up and see David re-enter the dining room with a look of pure venom on his face. "Cassie! Enough! No one said anything about forever."

"Yeah, you're right. You're absolutely right. Nothing is forever," I say very quietly. "Wow, all of a sudden I'm not feeling well. Will you please excuse me?" I say, looking at Sarah and Declan. I stand up and leave my plate on the table. I think I ate one bite, but that's all I can handle right now anyway. I smile at Sarah and Declan. They nod at me then turn to glare at their son. I walk to my bedroom, shut the door, and press the lock. Sitting on my bed, I wonder what my next move should be. Things with David have moved too fast. Sure, we've known each other ten years. It's just this notion that one minute he wants to be a couple, he says he loves me, and the next he can't think long-term. Well, neither can I.

23

CASSANDRA

HOME SWEET HOME

I spent the night in my own bed last night. I didn't leave my room even when David knocked and pleaded for me to come out to talk. "I'm sorry, Cassie," he murmured through my door.

I didn't give him the silent treatment. I responded, "I'm tired. Today was too much. I just want to get a good night's sleep."

I could hear the sigh on the other side of the door. "Okay. Sweet dreams, angel."

Angel? Sweetie? Baby? Honey? Big Ass? I can't seem to keep his terms of endearments from leaving a bad taste in my mouth. He's all sweetness when he's got me on all fours. When we're in public, it's different. I'm supposed to be the submissive there too, I guess. The thing is, David is going to have to accept that is *not* going to happen. I watched my mom lose herself in my dad. He's a good man, don't get me wrong, but he expected her to be home to cook for him and raise the kids while he worked the farm. She had a degree from Iowa State University. She had goals and dreams too. She just handled it all wrong, that's all. I bet she wishes she hadn't left us, but pride kept her away, and that's too bad for her. She missed out.

When the morning light touches my face, I sit up. I don't think I slept a wink. There's too much information running through my head. I hear his shower running as I look at my clock. "Seven." He should be out the door in thirty minutes. All I have to do is sit tight until he leaves. Then I can pack my bag and go home. A chill runs down my spine. A chill of excitement. All because I miss my house, my home. I saved up a hefty down payment before I started the house hunt. The minute I walked into the townhouse I now own, I knew. Even with the terrible décor, the dirty carpets, and the scuffed hardwood floors, *I knew*. It was a diamond in the rough, and it was all mine. Since then, I've slowly remodeled. The first order of business was the kitchen. I had the cabinets refaced, a new tile backsplash added, and granite countertops installed. The appliances were in okay shape, but they were black, so I traded those in on stainless steel. It wasn't cheap, but the way I did it was the most cost-effective way I could. The bathrooms were next. I did the same type of thing to the hall bathroom, but I gutted the master bath. I wanted the steam shower, the giant bathtub, double sinks, and new tile throughout. It's now a showstopper. I love, love, love my bathroom.

So, yeah, I miss my house. When I hear David walk past my door, I hold my breath. I listen as his footsteps pause right outside. I can just picture him standing there, weighing his options. Should he knock? Should he let me sleep? Luckily, he chooses the latter. I sigh in relief when he moves on. I tiptoe to the door and place my ear over it. I can hear him in the kitchen, no doubt making himself a cup of coffee—something I'd been doing for him the last few days.

I watch the clock. When it nears 7:30, I move to the door and open it a crack so I can listen for the door. When I hear the front door open then close, I wait a few minutes before I open my door, just to be sure. When I peek out, I see the coast is clear. Sighing, I step into the kitchen to grab a mug and see the note.

I'm sorry, Cassie. I was an ass. Forgive me? -D

I pick the note up and fold it in half, sliding it into the waist of my sleep shorts. Sipping my coffee, I start to pick up my things. I've left books, newspapers, hair ties, and lots of other things all over his place. "God, I'm a slob." I carry it all back to my room and set it on the dresser. I strip off the sheets for the laundry. I grab a second set of sheets I found in the hall closet and remake the bed. Mom always taught me a guest always picks up after herself. I lift up my suitcase and load everything inside. It's a tight fit, but I get it zipped up. Next, I bring up my Uber app and set up a pickup time for the early afternoon. I shower and change into clean clothes, toss the sheets into the washer, and take one last look around. Rolling out the door, I peek back one last time. I'll miss being here with him, but I need to be home.

24

DAVID

HONEY, I'M HOME.

It was hell, but I didn't let myself call or text Cassie today. I knew she needed time to forgive me. I'm an asshole. When I heard her tell my parents that, essentially, we were now a couple, I lost my shit. I wasn't ready for the world to know. And believe me, if you tell my mom anything, the world *will* know. Instead, I worked quietly in my office, doing my best to avoid every person in the place. At least, everyone that would let me. Gretchen interrupted my solitude so many times I'm positive I got nothing done. She had questions about everything, even questioning the number of copies she should make of a memo I needed to be sent out. My answer? "None. Email it. Why waste paper?"

"Oh, right." She had giggled.

The next few visits were just to see if I was hungry or thirsty or if I needed a break. "No," was my response all three times. She's never going to take the hint. I've accepted it now. The final time I nearly came unglued. I was in my bathroom sitting on my toilet when I heard the nob jiggle. Then a key slide into the lock. I watched with unblinking eyes as she opened the door and peeked her head in. "David?" She giggled.

"Get out of my bathroom, Gretchen. Jesus, I'm on the toilet."

"I don't mind," she says, stepping inside.

I place my hands over my privates and blink. I almost feel a tear—my eyes are burning. I know there's no video in the bathroom, but there's audio, so I make sure to enunciate every word. "Gretchen. Get out of my bathroom. Now! I'm taking the key away from you as soon as I'm done here. You're no longer allowed to use keys to enter my office or *private* bathroom." This is entirely inappropriate. Now, get out!" I shout.

"Fine," she says exasperatedly. "Whatever. You're no fun."

I know if I take her keys, she's just going to get another set, but I need to do it, and then I need to document it. If she finds another set of keys after I've asked her not to come into my office and bathroom, then that shows intent on her part.

I finish up, wash my hands, and walk into my office. When I step out, I see Lester sitting in my chair. A little startled, I say, "Lester. How are you?" I do my best to smile, but it's not happening. I remain in the doorway of the bathroom, hoping the audio device picks up this conversation, so I can have the best possible audio video for this conversation.

"I thought we should have a little chat."

"About?" This time I muster up a small smile.

"For starters, Gretchen. She said you're going to take her keys away."

"I am."

"You can't. She's got a set of master keys. I gave them to her. I want her to have them."

"Lester, she just came into my bathroom when I was sitting on the john. It's inappropriate."

"It was an accident. She said she wanted to make sure you had supplies stocked up in there. She didn't know you were in there."

"The door was locked."

Lester shrugs. "She keeps her keys."

"Fine. What else do you need?"

"What are your thoughts about Beranger Aeronautics?"

"Who?" Okay, acting dumb isn't the way to go, but I had to think fast.

"Oh, come now, son. I know you're aware they went public last week."

"I seem to recall something about that, but I haven't given them much thought."

"So, you didn't invest."

"No. I did not." I emphasized those last three words.

"Why not?"

I shrug. "Didn't feel right."

He lets out a scoff. "I thought you didn't rely on instinct. You're all about research."

"I use instinct all the time. I just merge it with research. In this case, I didn't feel it was a good bet."

"Hmm, interesting. All right, if that's how you want to play it." He chuckles. "I'll see you in the morning. Staff meeting."

I groan as soon as he leaves my office. I watch the door open back up, and Gretchen steps in with a look that tells me everything I need to know. She won that round, but fuck if I'm not going to win the war.

I look at my watch, and an idea hits me. I can kill two birds with one stone. "Gretchen, how'd you like to do a little shopping for me?"

She smiles so wide I think her skinny face may crack. "Of course. What do you need? A new tie?"

"No, I need a gift for my girlfriend."

"*Girlfriend?* Since when?"

I ignore her question. "Something pretty and sparkly, I think."

"Who is she?"

"Cassandra."

She coughs like she's about to choke. "Fat Cassandra?"

"Please don't call her that."

She lets out a laugh. "Why not? It's true. You could do *so* much better. I had no idea you were into fat chicks. But I guess I should have guessed it after seeing your ex-wife."

"Jesus. You women are terrible to each other. What about sisterhood and all that shit?"

Gretchen runs her fingers through her straight hair. "We have to look out for ourselves. No one else is gonna do it."

Oh, I think Lester is doing an excellent job looking out for Gretchen. Ending that conversation, I say, "Jewelry. A necklace, I think. Or earrings. Something classy and elegant." I reach into my pocket and pull out a credit card. "Please have it gift wrapped."

"Sure thing, boss." She grabs the card out of my hand and leaves.

"Finally. Peace and quiet."

Sitting back at my desk, I do a little research on Beranger. They haven't released any more information about the tech breakthrough, and people are starting to get a little worried. One reporter claims to have seen a personal demonstration while another article speculates that there's nothing behind the claims that they've revolutionized anything. I'm going with the latter claim.

As I'm clicking on a third story, my cell rings. I pick it up. "Mick, hey. What's up, little bro?" Mick is the youngest male in my family. My sister Emily is the baby. Mick started his own company, selling his own bottled alcoholic beverages. He calls his company Mick'sology. He's been in business less than a year, but his products are slowly gaining momentum. A few of the chain grocery stores in Chicagoland have picked him up, but he wants to go national. From time to time, he calls to ask my advice. I've never launched a new product, but I understand how business and the markets work. "Set a date yet?" Mick and Veronica—or Roni as we all call her—have been engaged for a few months now. Roni won't set a date, and it's making my brother uneasy.

"No, damn it. I'm just going to have to carry her to the justice of the peace one of these days or just do it in the backyard."

"I'll officiate." Why did I just say I'd do that?

"You will? That'd be amazing, Davie. Thanks. It's one less thing I need to worry about."

"How's the little guy?"

"C.J. is a spitfire, but you already knew that."

C.J. is his son, Calum Jeffrey. "He is. He reminds me of you when you were little. You were always getting into shit." I chuckle.

"Me? Nah, I was a perfect child. This is all Roni's fault."

We both laugh at that because it's pure bullshit. "How's business?"

"Ugh, slow. I need to figure out what I'm doing wrong, man. I was hoping by now I'd have at least made it up to Wisconsin. Those people love to drink."

"Patience. It'll happen. Have you considered bringing in another investor, a business partner who's more in tune with the grocery markets?"

"Not yet, man. For now, I want to keep this in the family. Roni's been doing a great job with marketing, but I need something big to happen."

"I get it. Let me roll it around in my head a little bit, see if I can come up with something."

"Sounds good. Best to Cassie." He snickers just as I hear the phone disconnect.

"Mom," I groan. See? She's already started spreading the word like a damn rash.

GRETCHEN FINALLY RETURNS five minutes before quitting time, thankfully. Her arms are full of packages that I'm sure I just paid for. I don't care. I had two hours of solitude. *Priceless.* She walks in and tosses a small square box at me that's wrapped in glittery gold paper. "Here you go. One gift for your girlfriend." She says "girlfriend" like she's talking about garbage.

Ignoring her, I reply, "Thank you. Have a good night."

She stomps out of my office, grabs the armload of shopping bags, and leaves. Shit, she's still got my credit card. Before I leave, I call my credit card company and ask them to freeze the account. If she tries to buy more stuff, she'll be declined. Serves her right. I work for a few more minutes, then grab the garishly wrapped gift as I leave. When I get to my condo, I pull my keys out and slide it into the lock. I open the door, setting down my briefcase. "Honey? I'm home." I chuckle at myself. Once I stop, I notice something strange. It's odd. All I hear is silence. No television, no stereo playing. I don't smell anything delicious cooking, and I can't really smell her anymore.

I step into the living room and see it's all tidy again. The throw that used to wrap around her as she read has been folded, and the pillows she'd lie back on are all where they're supposed to be. I quickly make my way to her bedroom and throw the door open. Empty. Her bed is made, and her suitcase is gone. I walk into the hall bathroom and see that her cosmetics are all gone too. No more Cassie. She's fucking gone.

My shoulders slump. "I did this. I fucked this up." I slowly make my way into the kitchen, where I see her note on the counter.

David,

Thank you for everything. I appreciate you taking care of me and keeping me safe. My lawyer called and informed me that Jennifer has been served with the restraining order. The initial court date on the assault charges is also set for two weeks from today. She's out on her own recognizance, but since she's been served, I feel it's safe enough for me to go home.

Take care, Cassie.

"Motherfucker." I'm still clutching the gift I bought her as I stomp back out my door. "The hell she is," I mutter. I jam my finger into the button on the elevator and wait. "That woman is going to be the death of me." I step onto the elevator and press the lobby button. It stops on three, and I watch as the blonde from a few weeks ago steps on with me. "Well, hello, Dave. How are you today?" she asks, getting so close to me I feel the need to back away.

"Fine. In a hurry to get to my girlfriend's place."

"Girlfriend? Well, that's a shame," she says, running her long fingernail down my tie.

"Not for me it isn't. I love her."

"Does that mean we can't play together?"

"Yes." I take her hand off my tie and push her away gently. "That's exactly what that means. I'm a one-woman man."

"Congratulations to you both, then." She smiles as she exits the elevator. I wait for a second or two before I step off. Outside, I flag down a cab. The ride gives me time to think. I use the time to wonder why she felt the need to sneak away like she did? Maybe she doesn't love me? She didn't say the words. "Damn. She doesn't love you back."

Before I knock on her front door, I give myself one more pep talk. "She does love me. I know she does. Hank said so." I knock once then hit the bell. I wait a minute then repeat.

"Coming."

I wait for the other three words.

"Who is it?"

"David."

Her groan is loud enough for me to hear. "Open up, honey. We need to talk."

The locks disengage, and the door opens. I step inside and notice how tired she looks. "You okay?"

"Yeah. Tired."

"We'll get to bed early tonight."

"David, I—"

"Shh, let's talk." I hand her the ugly gold box. "I bought you something. Picked it out special. I thought of you the minute I saw it." Yes, I know that's a lie.

"You didn't need to buy me a gift."

"I wanted to. Let's go upstairs, and you can open it."

I follow her into her little sitting room. She sits in her chair, and I sit on the sofa as close to her as I can get. She pulls the ribbon from the box and sets it on the table. She tears each side open then the back, giving me a smile as the paper falls to the floor. Looking down, she lifts the lid and gasps. She hasn't taken a breath yet, and her face has turned white as a ghost. Gretchen must have really picked out something great.

When she looks up, I decide that isn't the case at all. She, well, I don't know how to explain the expression. It's full of sadness and hate. Yeah, hate. "Why?" she asks, her voice sounds pained.

"Why did I buy you a gift?"

"Why did you do this to me? One minute you need me, the next you don't. One minute you think I'm sexy, the next you don't. One minute you say you love me, then you do this to me," she says, holding up the box. "I can't take it, David. I deserve better than this from you. I've stood by you through the good and bad. I've endured the rude things your wife has said to me and, hell, the things you've said to me. I deserve better than this." She holds up the box again. "If you think this is funny, you're dead wrong. I've lived my entire life hearing people comment about my body and my weight. Well, it's none of your fucking business any longer, David. I need for you to leave. *Now!* I want you out of my house, out of my life, and I want you to stay gone, David. Do you hear me?"

She stands and walks quickly down the steps to her front door. Kicking me out again? I follow her down because I've learned it's the best thing to do. She'll calm down. She hands me the box and opens the door. "Goodbye, David. And I mean it. *Goodbye.*"

I step out the door and hear it click closed behind me. I look at the box in my hand and want to throw it down the street, but I need to see what's inside. I pull open the lid and see a cheap plastic necklace like the ones you get out of a gumball machine. It's got a silver chain, but that's not the part that takes my breath away. It's the pendant. The pendant is a pig. A pig covered in cheap pink stones and one ruby for the eye. "Oh, God. I'm going to fucking annihilate Gretchen." I feel burning behind my eyes, then moisture. A tear runs down my cheek, and it's not the only one. "I've ruined everything. I love her so much it hurts." My tears turn into sobs. People are walking by staring, but I don't care. "I'll never get her back now." *It's over.*

25

CASSANDRA

A QUIET MAN IS USUALLY A THINKING MAN. A QUIET WOMAN IS USUALLY MAD.

As soon as he left, I sat down on my step. Twenty minutes. He's been gone twenty minutes, and I'm still sitting in the same spot because I'm stunned. I'm speechless. I'm shocked. I'm hurt. I'm angry, and I'm sad. Did he seriously think that necklace was the perfect gift for me? Is he completely and utterly clueless? Unfeeling? Insensitive? I guess the answer to all of those questions is yes.

But the man I know, the man I grew to love over the past ten years would never have given me such a thoughtless gift. He'd never pick that out for me. Granted, he's only ever given me utilitarian gifts like pens and travel mugs. This was his first attempt to give me something fit for a romantic relationship. Shit, I've gone out and purchased things for his wife before. He's handed me his credit card and said stuff like "Can you pick something pretty up for Jen? She's had a bad week. Maybe jewelry." Now, *that* makes more sense. Did he tell Jennifer he chose those gifts himself, so he'd get credit? Probably. Is that what he did this time? Did he let Gretchen choose my gift? I'll never know because I can't look at him. I can't let him break my heart again.

I make my way back upstairs. For some reason, I'm hungry. I

order a pizza from a nearby pizza place. When it's delivered, I sit on my comfy couch in my favorite room in the house, the sitting room, and turn on my recordings of the show *Playing House*. I need a laugh, and the ladies who write and star in the show never let me down. I consume almost the entire pizza, but that's okay. I've got no one to impress tonight or tomorrow or ever. After the show is over, I put my leftovers in the fridge and head up to bed. Not that I'll sleep. I won't, but I'll try. I can read for a while and see how it goes.

SHOCKINGLY, I wake up rested and rejuvenated in the morning. I guess that shot of whiskey I drank at three in the morning was the key. I add whiskey to my grocery list because I think I'm going to need it. I drink a cup of freshly brewed coffee and walk to my front door to get the papers. I pull it open a crack and nearly scream. A man is sitting on my front steps. "Declan! What are you doing here? How long have you been out here?"

"Not long, half an hour or so."

"What can I do for you?"

"Nothing. David mentioned you had a toilet that keeps running."

"He did?" I do have a toilet that keeps running.

"Um, yes. He did. I brought some tools," he says stiffly as he holds up a beaten-up old toolbox. Declan Flynn has his own construction company. A running toilet is child's play for a guy like him.

"Oh, okay. Come on in. Can I get you something to drink?"

"Coffee. Black, if you've got it. Also, point the way to the bathroom in question, please."

I lead him to the hall bathroom to the toilet that never stops making the sound of running water. I make my way to the kitchen and pull a cup down from the shelf. I'm almost out of coffee, so I jot that down on my grocery list and walk back to the bathroom. When I get there, he announces, "All done."

"All done? Seriously?"

Yep, your chain was just caught up on your tank lever. I untangled it. Now, you're good as new."

"Seriously? That's it? It's been running like that for weeks."

"Probably lost a lot of water too. Next time something's going on, give me a call. Okay?"

"Okay. Um, how much do I owe you?"

Declan chuckles. "Not a penny, sweetheart." He turns to walk down my hallway and turns back to me. "On second thought, I'd like one thing."

"Okay," I say cautiously.

"Hear him out. He screwed the pooch on this one, but he didn't mean to. He let that awful girl, Gretel, pick out the gift. He learned a valuable lesson yesterday. Just hear him out. My son is many things, but ungentlemanly is not one of them. I raised him better than that. Will you do that?"

"I'll think about it. No promises. But I'll think about it."

"That's good enough for me for now." He takes the cup from my hand and drinks the entire thing in one go."

"That was hot, Declan?"

He winks and leans down to kiss the top of my head as he hands me back the mug.

He's a man of few words. That's also hot. I giggle to myself as I think about how sometimes the best kind of man is a silent man.

26

DAVID

DRUNK IN LOVE. NOPE. JUST DRUNK. DEFINITELY JUST DRUNK.

Yep, that's what I am. Drunk. Just drunk. After leaving Cassie's, I called my dad. Declan Flynn is always the voice of reason. I told him everything, starting with Cassie quitting IIM and the reason why. I told him about our new relationship, leaving out the shit he doesn't need to know up until a few minutes ago when I handed my voluptuous woman a necklace with a pig on it. Dad listened. He was sympathetic to me once I finished, but he didn't try to sugarcoat things. "You screwed the pooch, David. Why would you let that assistant of yours buy a gift for your girl? That's a lazy-ass move, and the Flynns aren't lazy, son."

"I know, Dad. I was just trying to get some peace and quiet at work and get something for Cassie—kill two birds, you know?"

"You screwed the pooch."

"I know," I say, defeated. "I'm gonna get drunk."

"That's a terrific idea," Dad says sarcastically.

"It is. It's a fucking great idea." So, I stopped by the liquor store and bought a 750 ml bottle of Jameson Gold Reserve Irish Whiskey on my way home from Cassandra's.

In the morning light, I can now see the error of my ways. Drinking a bottle of whiskey wasn't one of my best and brightest ideas. The bottle is bone dry, so now I feel like someone has beaten me with a sledgehammer. Actually, I think I'd prefer being pummeled with a sledgehammer. It'd hurt less.

I slowly stand from my couch and take one step when the uncontrollable need to vomit hits me. I weave over to the large potted tree I've got in the corner, fall to my knees, and release the kraken. "Oh, God. I want to die. Kill me, please."

When no one grants me my wish, I crawl on my hands and knees over to the barstool near my kitchen. I use the rungs and the seat to pull me back up. Once I'm standing, I'm so winded I'm panting. My head hurts. "Damn." I look at the clock and see I've got about seven minutes until I need to be out the door for work. Not going to happen. I feel around my lower half for my phone, but I realize that I'm only wearing my boxers. I've got on my shirt, tie, and jacket but no pants. Classy. "Oh damn. Classy Cassie," I murmur. "My dad is right. I fucked the pooch." I can't decide if I want to cry like a pussy again or throw up. Ah hell. Why not do both?

I make it to the bathroom in the nick of time to relieve myself. I'm clutching the cool, white porcelain, liking how it feels on my face. I'm hot, and I stink like a frat house after homecoming weekend. I'll never make it to work on time. Where's my car? And how am I going to get to work? I can't find my phone. I have no idea where I left my pants. Oh wait! I remember now. I crawl back out into the living room and head to my tiny balcony. "Ah-ha!" I shout and regret it almost instantly. "My head," I moan.

I grab my pants and search the pockets. Thankfully, the phone is in the back pocket. I see I've missed a call from Mom and Dad, a text from Hank, and one from Mick. "They probably want to kick my ass too." Okay, that made no sense. I search for the contact information for that fucking bitch-face Gretchen and hit Send.

"IIM, this is Gretchen speaking."

"Gretchen? I'm sick. I'll... um, I'm gonna be late."

"You've got a meeting with Lest—I mean Mr. Ingot in fifteen minutes."

"Reschedule it. I'm going to be sick."

"He's going to be angry with you."

"Don't give a fuck." I hang up the phone and puke over the side of my balcony. "Please, God, don't let there be people below. Please?"

I fall back onto one of my two lounge chairs, hoping the sun will soak up the whiskey. When my phone rings, I look at the screen. "What?"

"Mr. Ingot is very displeased."

"Gretchen. The only person you need to worry about being displeased is me! And I'm very, very displeased with you."

"Why? What'd I do?"

"You bought my girlfriend a cheap necklace with a pig on it."

I hear her giggle. "Sorry about that. I couldn't resist."

"If I could fire you, I would. But, let me just say this, your days of working for me are over."

"But... what? You can't—" I don't let her finish.

I hang up the phone and plop back down on the lounge chair. When my cell rings again, I almost toss it over the railing, but when I see it's Lester, I pick up. "Hello?"

"Young man? You need to get your ass to work. We need to talk. Your attitude—"

"Lester, I'm sick. If you want me throwing up all over your desk, then, by all means, summon me."

"Fine. But I want to see you first thing in the morning."

"Fine." I hang up on the old man and seriously consider launching my cell out into oblivion, but I don't. What if Cassie calls?

27

CASSANDRA

A STRONG WOMAN IS ONE WHO IS ABLE TO SMILE IN THE MORNING LIKE SHE WASN'T CRYING LAST NIGHT.

Declan Flynn is a very clever man. He showed up in the guise of fixing my toilet, and in less than a paragraph, he said everything that needed to be said. He asked me to give David another shot. I will do as I promised; I'll think about it. Picking up my newspapers from the stoop, I head back into my sitting room, grabbing a fresh cup of coffee on my way through. I start with the Chicago Tribune, reading the arts and leisure section. I always start there. I mark down shows and exhibitions that I hope to see; then I go through the financial pages. I don't get far today when I read the headline:

Wall Street Stunned as New IPO Presents False Product Claims.

"Holy shit." I pull out the section and begin reading. "I knew it!" Beranger Aeronautics scammed millions, maybe billions of investors who thought they were on the ground floor of something huge. "I wonder if David saw this?"

I pick up my phone without thinking.

Me: Did you read the paper? *Headline: Wall Street Stunned as New IPO Presented False Product Claims.* Guess who that's about? I'm attaching the link.

I hit Send before I even consider what I've done. A day has gone by, and I no longer hold any anger toward him. I'm sad for him, really.

David: Holy shit! You were right! Not surprised. You know your stuff.
Me: Now, aren't you glad you didn't pour money into that deal?
David: Fuck yeah. I'd be broke. LOL.

I can't think of anything else to say, so I set my phone down until it chimes.

David: I'm very sorry. I let Gretchen pick that gift and have it gift wrapped. I had no idea what she'd purchased. I'd never hurt you like that.
Me: I know.
David: Is there hope for me? For us?
Me: Not sure. Still bruised a bit from yesterday. Give me some time.
David: I will. I will give you what you need.

That's our only conversation that day, but immediately afterward, I feel exhausted. Maybe having the weight of my anger off my shoulders made me sleepy. With that thought, I head back to bed to catch up on the beauty sleep I missed out on last night. As I lay my head down, the sentence that keeps running through on repeat is "I will give you what you need." The thing is, no matter how things went down yesterday, I can't help feeling hopeful. Hopeful that David Flynn meant what he said.

28

DAVID

THE THINGS TWO PEOPLE DO TO EACH OTHER THEY
REMEMBER. IF THEY STAY TOGETHER, IT'S NOT
BECAUSE THEY FORGET; IT'S BECAUSE THEY FORGIVE.

My day at home nursing this hangover is improved dramatically by that text from Cassie just now. *She texted me!* See? I knew I shouldn't throw my phone over the balcony! The crazy news about Beranger Aeronautics has me reeling. I never had any intention of investing in that company after seeing Cassie's doodles. True, I still had the article on my desk because, well, it's my desk. I've got shit on there from 2010. The big question remains, though. Why was Lester so interested in that article? And why did he have that little chat with me about Beranger the other day? Did he invest based on the notes from my desk? I sure as shit hope not. That'd be catastrophic.

With my hangover improved by at least 50 percent, I lumber into my bathroom for a much-needed shower. That will help me heal even faster. I scrub the stench of Irish whiskey off my body with vigor. "I'm never drinking again," I murmur as I feel my headache wane just a bit. "Swear to God. Never again." I know. Empty promises. The shower was a good idea, but a fresh bout of nausea is upon me. I lie on my bed and sigh. "Cassandra." I roll over to my side and mumble to myself, "How did you get under my skin after all these years? Why hadn't it happened sooner?" Ten years together and I couldn't see the nose on my face. I roll onto my back, close my eyes, and fall asleep in a matter of minutes.

I WAKE UP A LITTLE DISORIENTED. I look at the clock and see the glowing numbers. "6:00?" Is that morning or night? I passed out on my bed midafternoon. I sit up and see the morning sun shining in my window. Jesus, I slept over eighteen hours. My headache is gone, and I feel like I'm going to live. *Yay*. It's too bad I've got to go to work again. I slide out of bed and head to my kitchen to make coffee. It actually sounds good this morning. Once that's percolating, I make my way to the bathroom. The man looking back at me in the mirror looks a little like a lumberjack. "I need a haircut." Searching through the drawers, I find my razor and shaving cream. After a clean shave, I step in and shower quickly then dress in my best suit because it feels like a brand-new day. I make my way into the kitchen and pour coffee into Cassie's Chicago Bears travel mug. On the way out, I grab my briefcase and try to force positivity by sing-songing, "It's going to be an awesome day!"

By the time I get to my office, that lofty idea of an awesome day has been run over by a Mack truck. Hell has fucking broken loose. I was only gone one day. One. Day. My desk phone is blinking with messages that should have been taken care of by my worthless assistant. A quick glance at my work email, I see I've got over fifty emails, all with tiny red flags next to them telling me they're urgent. When I attempt to give my colleagues a cheerful, "Good morning!" none of them will look at me. "I had a fucking hangover people, get over it," I mutter.

"There's more to it than that," says a voice at my door.

"Oh, hey, Janice. What's up?"

She turns her head to the side, giving me a peculiar look. "I came to get you. H.R. wants to see you. Now."

Since I haven't even had a chance to sit down, I walk toward her. "What's going on? What's this about?"

"Can't say, confidential."

I groan but follow Janice. "Can I have a little hint?"

She looks back at me. "One word. Gretchen. Got your notes?"

"Fuck." I nod and pat my breast pocket for my notebook and my inside pocket for my phone. I've got my notes and so much more.

We take the elevator down to the first floor. Janice leads me along the corridors until I'm standing in front of the human resource director's office. I knock. "Come in."

I step in and see Jodi Flagg sitting behind her desk. She's got stacks of folders and papers all over the place. Her desk could rival mine for the most disastrous organization. "Jodi. Hey." Jodi and I go way back. She was my contact when I was first hired here. She did all of my paperwork for insurance and other benefits. She's also a friend of my sister Sandy. They've been tight for years. I've got no need to worry. She won't screw me over.

"David? Someone has lodged a complaint against you."

I nod. "What kind of complaint?" I know exactly who did this and why.

She clears her throat. "Sexual harassment."

"Gretchen?"

"I can't say. But I can give you the list of occurrences."

Janice slides a piece of paper toward me that's been neatly printed. The only problem? There are typos running throughout the document. "Only Gretchen would present a document with so many mistakes," I grumble. I read through the list, and I nearly choke.

- Contantly touching me.

That should be Constantly not *Contantly*.

- Says inappropriate things to me like wanting me to be in a sex sandwich with his brother.

I scoff at that one. A sex sandwich? That was all her.
"You think this is funny, Dave?" asks Jodi.
"Kind of. Yeah. She's talking about Hank and me." I continue reading her list.
"Jesus," she sputters. Jodi knows Hank. She loves my brother, thinks he's the most loyal and protective husband she's ever seen. So, she knows Hank would never make a "sex sandwich" with anyone but his wife.

- Walked in on my while I was in the shower. (*my?*)
- Walked in on me when I was using the restroom.
- Always asking me to work late, so we're alone.

I can't read the rest of the list because it's complete and utter bullshit. "This is total and complete bullshit."
Jodi looks over her glasses at me. A look that says... prove it.
"I've got proof."
Jodi's expression changes quickly to surprise. "I've got documentation." I pull out my little notebook with every date and time that she touched me, said dirty shit to me, and walked into my bathroom.
Jodi takes the book from my hand. "She's got a similar list. This isn't going to be much help. She's Lester's niece."
"Yeah, well how 'bout audio and video?"
Jodi's face lights up, and there's a slight smile forming on her lips. "You've got video?"

"Hank set it up. Janice warned me that she might do this."

Barely audible, I hear Jodi mumble, "Thank fuck." She clears her throat and adds, "Can I get copies of everything?"

Sure thing. I pull out my phone and access the app. It allows me to forward the footage to email. I select all the video files and email them to Jodi. "The bathroom was audio only for obvious reasons. The recorder for that is in my bathroom. I can download the audio files for you as soon as I get back upstairs."

Jodi has already opened her email and has clicked on the first video. "What's Lester doing going through your desk?"

"I don't know. That was weeks ago. If you keep watching, he takes pictures of some of my papers as well."

"Interesting."

I watch her click her mouse on other files. She nods and smiles throughout. "This is unbelievable. I've had it with her. You're the third guy she's accused. You're the first to have proof she's full of shit. Do I have your permission to keep these and use them as needed?"

"You do."

"Go back to work. I'll be in touch." She turns back to her screen. "Oh, and get me the audio from the bathroom."

"I will."

As I leave her office, I hear her pick up her phone. "Gretchen? I need you in my office. Now."

I didn't see her upstairs. I wonder where's she's hiding now.

Back in my office, I look at the mess on my desk and sigh. "This is the last place I want to be." I pull my phone out of my jacket and send a text to Cassandra.

Me: I know I told you I'd give you time, but can you meet me for lunch? Things are going down here at work, and I need a confidant.

I don't have to wait long.

Cass: Sure. Doc B's? Noon?
Me: Perfect. C U there.

I love that place, and Cassandra knows it. Their wedge burger is better than sex. Well, it used to be better than sex until I had sex with Cassie. Nothing is better than sex with Cassandra Darrow. Shit, I'm getting a hard-on. I've gotta stop thinking about Cass and wedge burgers.

29

CASSANDRA

LIFE IS NOT ABOUT WHO'S REAL TO YOUR FACE. IT'S ABOUT WHO'S REAL BEHIND YOUR BACK.

Meeting David for lunch is probably a bad idea. I'm not ready to jump back into bed with him. I'd like to, but that would be too hasty, and... he's still got some groveling to do, because honestly, I'm still a little wounded. I know I'll get over it. I always get over it, but I'm not ready to forgive and forget just yet. I get to Doc B's twenty minutes early so I can get a table. During the lunch hour, it's nearly impossible, but I only have to wait fifteen minutes. I text David to let him know I've got a table, and then I check the updates on my favorite financial websites. I've set up a filter that will flag any articles related to Beranger. When I click open my browser, there are at least twenty new articles listed.

I scan to a new headline.

Beranger Aeronautics Lies Cause Losses in the Millions for Chicago-based companies.

I read through the article, looking for the names of companies and analysts who have been affected. When I see Ingot Investment Management listed, I freeze. David's name is listed in the article. "What the hell?"

"Hey, Cass. What's wrong?" David says as he sits.

"Read this!" I hand him my phone and watch. He said he didn't invest, but maybe he changed his mind and did invest after all.

"What the fuck is this!" he shouts. He looks over at me. "This is bullshit. Who wrote this fucking piece of shit?"

"Calm down, David. Here, give me my phone." I scroll to the top of the story and read the byline. I do an internet search for the Tribune's phone number. I hit the number and wait. "Yes, may I speak to Kevin Ross?"

David's face is a bright shade of red. His leg is bouncing up and down so fast the table is vibrating. "David, we'll get to the bottom of this."

When I hear a masculine voice answer, I focus on the call. "Kevin Ross? Yes, my name is Cassandra Darrow. I'm David Flynn's assistant. We just read your article." He interrupts me, but I keep talking. "We just read your story, and you're going to need to print a retraction."

I lean in close to David, so he can hear Kevin Ross. I'd love to put him on speakerphone, but the restaurant is packed. The reporter sputters. "Retraction? Why?"

"Because Mr. Flynn did not invest in Beranger Aeronautics."

"According to his *actual* assistant, he did." Uh-oh, busted already.

"Do you have a name?"

"Confidential source."

"Well, I guess you give us no recourse, his attorney—"

"Wait! Are you saying he really didn't invest?"

"That's exactly what I'm saying. You were given false information—information that will have a detrimental impact on Mr. Flynn's business. I believe they call it defamation, or is it libel?"

"I've got a memo signed by David Flynn."

"A memo?" I look at David, and he shakes his head. "Mr. Flynn believes you were provided with a forged document."

"Jesus," Ross mutters. "Just what I need."

"If you'd like to interview Mr. Flynn to get the story straight—" I look up and see David nod his head. "—we'd be happy to set that up with you, but it would need to be done today and printed as a retracted statement from your editor tomorrow at the latest. An online retraction published today would be preferable."

"Fine. I'll call you back. This a good number?"

"It is. Oh, and, Mr. Ross?"

"Yeah."

"We'll need a copy of that memo."

"I'll have to clear that with my boss. I'll let you know."

I press the red button and look over at David. "This is getting interesting."

"If you call having your career shoved down the toilet by a vindictive secretary, then yeah, it's interesting." He grabs his napkin and sets it in his lap. "Let's eat. I need food. I haven't eaten for almost two days. Besides, I wanted to see you." He smiles softly. "I've missed you. I'm so sorry about the other night."

"I know." But I'm not ready to forgive entirely. I'm working on it.

The server arrives, and David orders his burger with sweet potato fries. I order the Black Tiger Shrimp Salad. After the server leaves, I feel a hand over mine. He's leaned over the table and placed his big hand over my smaller one. "I mean it, Cassie. I'm sorry."

I nod. "I know."

Over lunch, David tells me about Gretchen's attempt to pin a sexual harassment claim on him. "You showed the videos to Jodi?"

"I did. I also sent her the audio from the bathroom."

We stop talking as the server sets down our food. When she steps away, I look over at him. "I can't believe all this is happening, David. What happened to IIM?"

"Gretchen happened, and I think Lester happened."

"Funny you should mention Lester."

"Yeah?" he asks, leaning forward.

"Before I quit, there was a rumor going around about him. As a rule, I ignore rumors, but now that this has come up, I think it might be relevant."

"Rumors?"

"You know, rumors the assistants were talking about." I take a sip of my water. "Anyway, the talk was that Lester was losing his touch. The board of directors has been pressuring him to either step aside as president and chairman and retire, or get to work landing some huge deal."

He nods as he bites into his burger. "Makes sense. I don't remember the last time Lester scored big."

I nod too. "What if Lester is the one who lost money?"

"That might make sense, and it bears out my theory that I'm being set up."

"Would he go that far to pin this on you? There's a digital trail for every transaction. You have to use your broker user name and I.D. to make any purchases or trades."

He stops chewing. "Motherfucker."

"What?"

"I keep all of my passwords in that desk drawer. They're locked up, but that wouldn't stop Lester or Gretchen."

"Did you find any footage of them looking into your desk drawers?"

He pulls out his phone and presses a few things. "There's a lot on here I haven't seen yet. Housekeeping triggers it all the time—I stopped reviewing the footage." His fingers marched over his phone. "I'm going back to when Beranger went public."

I am picking up my fork when he growls. "Mother-cock-fucker."

I set my fork down. "What?" He shows me the screen. Gretchen and Lester are picking the lock on his bottom desk drawer. Once they get in, they dig around until they find his small password book. They leaf through it and then start to snap pictures. "Have you checked your accounts lately, David?"

"Not in the last couple of days. But...." He raises his finger. "None of my personal account passwords are in that book. The only thing in there relates to client accounts."

"That's enough. He could have cleaned out everyone you represent."

"Mother-son-of-a-fucker," he growls. "This is getting serious."

"We need to do two things right away. Get the retraction printed and hack into the computer system. They'll have left a lovely trail of breadcrumbs. It won't be difficult to turn that into a paper trail. It's too bad we don't know a computer genius." I smirk at David with raised eyebrows. We *do* know a computer genius.

"Ernie. We'll call Ernie . He'll be able to find what we need."

I smile encouragingly. "Call him. The sooner he can get what we need, the better off you'll be. Because, David, right now, your goose is cooked."

He looks over at me. "It is, isn't it?"

I nod. "It is."

30

DAVID

EVEN IF YOUR GOOSE HABITUALLY LAYS GOLDEN EGGS, IT WILL STILL BE COOKED.

Over lunch, Cassandra and I work out a game plan. She'll go home and gather up all the research she's done on Beranger. I'll head back to the office to get the newspaper article about the IPO with her illustrated notations in the margins and dig around my desk for anything else that might be pertinent.

I'll also call my cousin Ernie Flynn before I get back to the office. Ernie's a computer nerd of the highest order. He's actually a little socially awkward, but if you saw him in a room full of Flynn men, you'd never notice because he blends in seamlessly with us since we all resemble our identical twin fathers. But, unlike the other Flynn men, the guy knows *everything* about computers. He can program them, and he can hack them. He's a genius. We're going to be very stealthy about this. I don't want a federal hacking conviction, or charge, on my resume.

I press his name on my contacts list. "Yeah?"

I chuckle. "I don't get a greeting? Just 'yeah'?"

"Yeah. What's up, cuz?"

No need to beat around the bush. "I need a big favor. The kind of favor that we keep between us."

"Uh, are you into drugs or something? I don't read minds. What do you need?"

"Can you meet me in an hour? It's a conversation that we should have in person. Not on the phone."

"Jesus," he grumbles. "Yeah. Okay. Where?"

"Starbucks on Hubbard and North Clark. By your office."

"Okay."

He hangs up. Apparently, this conversation has ended.

I jog down the block toward IIM. I want to get in and get out without seeing Lester or Gretchen. When I get off the elevator, I'm shocked at how quiet it is, and it's only two o'clock. I practically slither into my office and quietly shut the door, locking it behind me. At my desk, I find the article first. I check through my papers to find anything else that might help us.

I don't see anything out of the ordinary until I get halfway through the stack of papers. "What the hell is this?"

It's a memo, supposedly from me to Lester, dated the day before Beranger went public.

> **IIM**
> Ingot Investment Management
>
> **Memorandum**
>
> To: Lester Ingot
> From: David Flynn
> Date: June 19
> Re: Beranger Aronautics IPO
>
> Lester,
> You've been such a wonderful mentor for me. I think of you like a father. Because of everything you've done for me over the years. I wanted to let you know I've done extensive research on Beranger Aronautics. As you know, they're going to the stock market tomorrow. Now's the chance for us to really make a big splash for IIM and take us into the new millenuam. I hope you'll see what I see and invest heavily in Beranger.
>
> Sincerly,
> Your friend,
> David

"Holy shit. Where do I start with this piece of crap?" First, there are so many spelling errors, I know it was written by Gretchen. *'They're going to the stock market tomorrow?'* Agitated, I run my fingers through my hair. I can't believe what I'm seeing. I quickly make several copies of the memo. On one of the copies, I highlight the multiple errors. "Ever heard of spell-check, Gretch? Jesus, this is fucking embarrassing."

I grab the digital recorder from the bathroom, my laptop, my keys, the memos, and the newspaper with Cassie's notes. As I pass Gretchen's desk, I see her IIM laptop sitting open on her desk. I grab that as well. Technically, she works for me—I have a right to check that she's doing the stuff I ask her to do. Right?

I'm about to turn the corner toward the elevators when I hear Lester. "Fuck." I duck into an alcove obscured by a tall bookcase. I hold my breath, listening.

"I know. I know. This is serious. I had high hopes for the boy, but he's put us in a very compromising position. He'll go before the board; I'm afraid there will be serious consequences." Lester, the asshole, sounds sad and betrayed.

"Should we notify the Securities and Exchange Commission? He may have violated more than our trust." Pete Valley, vice chairman of the board of directors, sounds very serious.

"I'm afraid we may have to call them. Sad, sad state of affairs." The lying sack of shit, Lester Ingot, makes a tsk-tsk noise. What a piece of work he is.

The voices get quieter. They've moved down the hall and into the conference room. I hear the door to the conference room click closed. I duck out of the niche and race to the elevator. I hit the down button but quickly decide the stairs are safer. I push through the door to the stairs and start taking the steps down, two at a time. I feel winded after the first flight. "Shit. I need to get to the gym."

I beat Ernie to the Starbucks. I'm working on a list of priorities when I get a text from Cassie.

Cassie: Kevin Ross called. Meeting set up with Ross and editor for 5 p.m. tonight.
Me: Got it. Waiting for Ernie at Starbucks on Hubbard and North Clark.
Cassie: On my way.

Great. Ernie is going to respond much better to her. She has such an easy way with people; she always seems to charm anyone she comes across. That's a talent that I definitely don't possess.

31

CASSANDRA

...AND IT'LL BE JUST LIKE OLD TIMES.

Walking into David's place feels a little surreal. It wasn't that long ago that I stayed here, but it feels like a long time. I suck in a deep breath, trying to ignore the current of feelings I'm experiencing, and head into the dining area. "Should we work here?" I ask before I sit down.

"Sure. Good idea. Need anything? Are you hungry?"

"No, I'm not hungry. Just water, please."

Coming around the corner from the kitchen, David has already pulled off his jacket and tie. He hands me the bottled water and opens one for himself as he sits down. "Ernie was able to get us into Lester and Gretchen's email accounts. So, where should we start?" he asks, sifting through the prints of Lester's emails.

"Lester's emails. But I think we should see what he's been up to today."

"Agreed." David opens up the IIM web mail server and types in Lester's username and password. He turns the laptop to me, so we can view his account together.

"Wow, he's been busy," I deadpan.

"He certainly has. I need to check my own email. I have a

feeling I'm going to be summoned to an emergency board meeting." David opens up another window on his browser. He types in his username and password, and sure enough, he's got emails from the chief financial officer of IIM and the vice chairman of our board of directors, Peter Valley. "They want to see me today."

"Well, I think you need to get your ducks in a row before meeting with them. You need to have the truth and the proof before you meet with them."

"I agree. I'll reply, but I'll be vague." As he types, I sort through the emails, putting them in order chronologically. "I told them I was out of the office and have an appointment at five. Let's see what they do with that."

"Good. Okay, I've got these in order. I'll read through them and put together a summary for you. You go through his other emails to see what we're actually dealing with here."

David nods.

We work in companionable silence for a good thirty minutes, and it feels just like old times. It's how we have always worked together. It feels natural. I break the quiet by saying, "Wow, the two of them are something."

"Who? Lester and Gretchen?"

"Yeah. I actually think he knew she set up his vice presidents for sexual harassment. He doesn't come right out and say it, but he alludes to it."

"Not surprising. He's gotten himself into a fucking mess," David says, pointing to his screen. "Going back to the day before Beranger went public, he was trying to scrounge up a bunch of cash. He's dragged some big names into this thing. I wouldn't be surprised if he brought his own company down with the amount of money he put on this thing. It looks like two point five million dollars."

"Why? Why would he do that? Did he base this entirely on

the scribbles on that newspaper?" I ask, pointing to my doodles. "If so, he's lost his touch."

"He's definitely lost his touch. My name is mentioned in almost all of these emails. People thought I had the scoop on this deal, and he was promoting it based on that." David pulls his laptop closer to himself and types. "Oh, here we go."

"What?" I stand and walk to the other side of the table, so I can see what he's got on his screen.

David places his palm on my hip and nudges me closer to the table and his computer. "They want to see me after my appointment."

"Well, that's interesting," I say sarcastically. I stand and peer down at him. He looks good—with his longer hair and his five o'clock shadow. "Are you ready to meet with them?

I'm staring at him. He looks up at me, and before he speaks, I feel his palm make small circular movements on my hip almost absently. "Probably not, but I'd rather get it over with, truthfully."

"I get that." I can't say more because his hand has slowly moved around to my ass. When my eyes meet his, his expression has changed from distracted to seductive. His irises are dilated, and the bright blue has turned dark. I take a breath.

His other hand moves to the other hip, and he pulls me to him until I'm standing between his legs. "I've missed you, Cassie. Say you forgive me, *please*?" He actually sounds a little desperate.

"I forgive you."

He moves his right hand up until it's at the back of my neck. He's gently nudging me forward. Just as he's about to kiss me, I add, "But, if you ever have your assistant buy me a gift again, I'm done."

I can tell he thinks I'm kidding, but when he sees my expression, his smile disappears. He looks at me sincerely. "I won't. I promise."

I bend down but stop short before I kiss him. I look at him seriously. "I mean it, David. You're going to need to treat me with kid gloves for a while. I'm not that confident in your ability to not screw this up."

This time he laughs. "Jesus, babe. Of course, I'll screw this up. You know me, right? It's not in my DNA to be smooth. I'm going to fuck up. Please, keep that in mind." He slides his lips over mine, back and forth. As he sucks my bottom lip into his mouth, I feel my nipples bead. I open my mouth and lick his top lip.

"Fuck, Cassie. I need to touch you."

"We don't have time. It's—" I don't get the rest of my words out because he's kissing me again. His hands slide up my outer thighs, lifting my skirt as they go. "David?" I pant.

"I know." He rests his forehead against mine. His breath is evening out. "We need to focus on this. But promise me, Cassie...."

I'm not sure I can make promises, but I wait to hear what he has to say.

"Will you stay with me tonight?"

He's asking me instead of telling me. It's a change and one I appreciate. "I will."

"Good." He sighs with relief. "I need you in my arms after all of this today."

I smile but then step back. "Let's finish up here. We need to leave for our meeting at the Trib soon."

"Right."

32

DAVID

THREE THINGS CANNOT BE LONG HIDDEN: THE SUN, THE MOON, AND THE TRUTH.

We walk to the Tribune building, holding hands. The Trib is only a few blocks from my place, so we arrive fifteen minutes early. On the building directory, the finance section should be on the seventh floor. Since nobody can just walk into the Tribune office, we stop at the security desk and tell them we have an appointment with Kevin Ross. The guard makes a call, and when he hangs up, he hands each of us a visitor pass and gives us directions to the reporter's office.

I'm fidgeting in the elevator. That's not typical behavior for me—I'm normally pretty confident and cool, but this thing has caused me to lose some of my mojo. I feel a small hand squeeze mine. I turn and smile at my beautiful girl. "It's going to be okay," she says sweetly. "You've got this." She runs her hand down my tie and tugs slightly. "You've got on your lucky tie. Nothing bad can happen when you're wearing this tie, right?"

"You're right." Cassie suggested I change into my lucky tie before we left my place. "Thanks for thinking of it." I smile back at her as the doors open. "Here we go." I squeeze her hand before I let it go.

At reception, I ask for Kevin Ross. We're directed to a large, glass-walled conference room. The room is empty as we enter. We sit next to each other and face the large newsroom. It's like watching a movie scene. People are bustling around at a frantic pace; probably working on last-minute stories for the next edition.

"Busy place." Cassie is reading my mind.

"Hectic, but I bet it's never dull. I—"

The door opens, and a man and woman walk in. The woman looks about my age and the guy about Cassie's age. We both stand. I hold my hand out to the man. "You must be Kevin. David Flynn." I turn to Cassie and start to say, "This is Cassandra Darrow, my—"

"Business partner," she finishes.

I blink at her, and for the first time in our tenure, I see her as exactly that, my partner—in everything.

The woman with Kevin raises her hand to me. "Chastin Caverly. Editor." She shakes Cassie's hand then adds, "Nice to meet you, Cassandra."

"Caverly? Do you know a Malcolm Caverly?" asks Cassie.

"I think I do." Chastin smirks. "He's my son."

"Wow, really? We went to Loyola together. I love Malcolm." She *loves* Malcolm? *Who the fuck is Malcolm?*

"How is he?" Cassie asks, interrupting my jealous thoughts.

"He's terrific. He's got a son who's almost three and another baby on the way. Crossing fingers it's a girl." She winks. "I can't wait to buy some of those adorable dresses."

"I know what you mean." Cassie chuckles. "I'm so happy for him. Tell him I said hello, would you?"

As long as that's the only thing she does. Cassie doesn't need to be rekindling any relationship with Malcolm Caverly. No way.

"I sure will, Cassandra." Chastin pauses and leads us back to the table. "Let's get started. Tell me why you're here."

Cassie begins, "We're here to clear David's name and to give you an important story. If you agree to print a retraction." Cassie turns to look at Kevin as she continues. "David's career may be irreparably damaged by your reporting, Kevin. Did you try to contact David to interview him?"

Kevin looks at me. "Uh, I called your office. Your secretary told me you didn't want to speak to the newspaper."

I start to sputter, but Cassie goes right on talking to Kevin. "You made one attempt to speak to him? It doesn't sound to me like you did your due diligence. He's got a landline at his home with a listed number. Did you try to call his home? Did you email him? Did you search for him on Twitter, Facebook, or Instagram?" She's looking at Kevin with the fiercest expression I've ever seen.

"Uh, no."

Cassie doesn't stop there. "Because, Kevin, if you had done your due diligence, you would have discovered some serious discrepancies with Gretchen Ingot's story."

"Gretchen Ingot?"

I finally speak. "Yes. She's Lester Ingot's niece."

Chastin looks at Kevin, and she doesn't look happy. She looks back at me. "Okay." She sighs. "Let's see what you've got; then we can talk about our next step."

Cassie and I pull out the printouts showing the emails between Gretchen and Lester. We also show her Lester's emails that are dated around the time of the IPO of Beranger Aeronautics.

Chastin's expression is grim. She sifts through the stack of papers. "Do I want to know how you got these?" She's looking at both Cassie and me.

I speak first. "No."

"Shit," she mutters. "So, what you're saying is that Lester

used information that he took from your desk without your permission."

"Misinformation," I correct her.

"Right. Misinformation. He then took that info—misinformation—and invested heavily in Beranger Aeronautics. When the shit hit the proverbial fan, he turned this around to be your fault."

"In a nutshell, yes," I reply. "Here, let me show you this." I pull out my phone and bring up the app for my office videos." This is Lester sitting at my desk. He was waiting for me as I exited my bathroom. Watch this."

We wait as Chastin and Kevin watch the exchange about Beranger and hear why David hadn't invested. It's partial proof that David was smart enough to stay away from that IPO.

"Interesting," says Chastin. "What about the memo?"

We both laugh when she mentions Gretchen's handywork. "That was all Gretchen. The woman can't spell. I've got memos saved showing other examples."

"I'm not gonna lie, I was a little concerned that you had written that memo," laughs Kevin. He really doesn't have any reason to laugh. He royally fucked this thing up.

I ignore the dumbass Kevin and show them two more videos. The first video shows Lester searching my desk, and the second one is of Gretchen and Lester breaking into my drawer to access passwords.

"Our reporting estimates he invested over two million. Have you heard anything on your end?"

"No. I've been asked to meet with the board of directors tonight, though. I may know something after that."

"The board? Why?"

"For the same reason I'm here now. They think this was my doing."

Chastin stands. "I'll post something in our online addition, but we'll print a retraction in the morning. We're going to follow up on this information and do real research." Chastin pointedly looks at Kevin before turning back to me. "May I make copies of these emails?"

"Those copies are for you."

"I'd love the full scoop about this when the dust settles—if you'll give it to me. I'll be sure you're the hero and not the villain," Kevin says.

Cassie and I look at each other then back at Kevin. "He *is* the hero in all of this," Cassie says determinedly.

"Right. Of course, Cassandra. I didn't mean anything...."

"It's okay," I respond. "We can talk when we both know more. We'll see ourselves out." I take Cassie by the hand and lead her out through the newsroom and into the elevator. Once inside, I lean down and kiss her lips. "You were amazing in there."

"Thanks." She smiles up at me.

"For the record, I loved the sound of Cassandra Darrow and David Flynn, business partners."

She smiles up at me again. "We did make a great team. It's a shame you screwed the pooch on that." She's laughing as she says it.

I groan. "I know. *Believe me*, I know! But we shouldn't give up on the idea of working together again. We'd be unstoppable."

Nodding, Cassie squeezes my hand. "Maybe that's just the job opportunity I've been waiting for—as long as we're equal partners. I'm not going back to being your administrative assistant."

"Of course not. If we work together again, it's as partners. Equals." I lean down to kiss her again and smile, thinking of one word: *Wife*.

33

DAVID

KARMA HAS NO MENU. YOU GET SERVED WHAT YOU DESERVE.

Outside the Tribune building, Cassie and I part ways. We've already planned to meet at her place after the board meeting. I'll call her to say I'm on the way, and she's going to order takeout. It feels and sounds really domestic, and I've gotta say, I don't hate it.

Before she leaves, I kiss her lips and then her beauty mark for good luck. I don't think I need my tie now that I've got her for luck, but it doesn't hurt to double up on my luck today. Walking toward the office, I email Peter Valley to let him know my meeting is over. In minutes he responds, "We're in the large conference room next to Lester's office. See you soon."

"Shit. I'm nervous as hell."

I hit my Favorites and select Sandy's number. When she answers, I tell her, "Sandy? I need some encouragement. I'm about to walk into the lion's den."

"Huh? What are you talking about? I'm lost."

As I'm walking, I tell her all about my work drama.

"Jeez, dude. You should just quit that job. It sounds toxic."

"Strange. I had always pictured myself at IIM forever. Until all of this shit hit the fan. Now, I can't think about staying there one more day without getting nauseous."

"There are lots of other things a guy like you could do for a living. You could help Mick with Mick'sology. If you two hooked up, things would actually start happening."

"Damn, I never considered that." It would be great to work on a project like that, to nurture something and watch it grow. I bet Cassie would be a fantastic partner on that project too. The four of us, Roni, Mick, Cassie, and me—we'd be unstoppable.

"Maybe you should. If this meeting goes as badly as I think it's going to go, it's an option."

"I like options." For the first time since my promotion, I feel a sense of relief and hope. I smile into the phone. "God, I love you, Sandy. You're the best."

"Ah, you're so sweet. You owe me, asshole. Dinner and something real pretty from Crate and Barrel."

"All right. We'll go shopping next week." My sister loves home décor. She dabbles in interior design, but her real job is a self-employed digital strategist. She helps clients with their web presence, tweaking social media, making their company websites more streamlined and analyzing demographic data. It sounds pretty fancy, and she's really good at it.

"Sweet. Okay. Good luck and call me when you're done with the inquisition. I've got a meeting in a few minutes. If you get my voice mail, leave me a detailed message. Okay?"

I groan. "Okay." In the elevator, I try my best to keep my nerves in check. Thinking of working with Mick and Cassie helps. It's a good feeling to have an out. If this meeting goes down the way I think it will, I'll need an exit plan.

I knock on the conference room door. Peter Valley calls, "Come in."

I step inside and see angry faces sitting around the table.

Lester sits front and center, and he looks very smug. Peter Valley's expression is neutral.

I nod coolly and ask, "You wanted to see me?"

"You could say that," mumbles Peter. He looks at Lester who nods like a king on his fucking throne. Peter turns back to me. "We're not sure where to start, Dave. You seem to have fucked us all over."

"How so?" I say, pretending to be calm.

Insincere chuckles come from around the room, and they don't sound at all jovial.

"You advised Lester, all of your clients, and all of *his* clients to invest heavily in Beranger Aeronautics."

"That's not true."

Pete scoffs. "We have the paper trail to prove it, David. Funny. You didn't invest any of your own money."

"Funny," I deadpan.

"Son, this is deadly serious. I don't appreciate your smart-ass attitude," growls Lester.

"And I don't appreciate getting set up to take the fall, *sir*." I say "sir" with venom.

"Well, I never...," sputters Lester.

"Well, there's a first time for everything," I say, obviously mocking the man.

"Enough!" shouts Peter. "You're making a serious accusation, David. We've got the proof, with this memo that you advised Lester to—"

"That memo was forged. I can spell. Gretchen, Lester's niece, cannot."

"She's your assistant, boy. You told her to write it up."

"Boy? Do you realize how demeaning that is?" *Old man*. That's what I'd like to say, but I hold my tongue. Lester tries to speak again, but I interrupt, "I've got proof."

Lester lets out a cracking laugh. "Proof? What kind of proof?"

"Video." I watch as Lester's face pales to a deathly shade of yellow. The guy must have liver problems.

"What do you mean you have video? Of what?" he sputters.

I turn to Peter. "I have one video of Lester going through my desk when I was gone. There's another video of Gretchen and Lester breaking into my locked drawer—the drawer that holds my passwords and client files, and I have a third video of Lester asking me if I had invested in Beranger."

Lester interrupts. "Well, that means nothing. Peter just told us you hadn't invested yourself."

"I also have emails between Lester and Gretchen."

"Emails!" Lester squeaks. "How in the fuck did you get emails?"

"My secretary isn't very careful." Ah-ha! That was pretty ingenious on my part. They won't suspect hacking if I go this route. "I took Gretchen's laptop for safe keeping. She'd left it open after leaving for the day. Very irresponsible. There are things on our computers that we wouldn't want to fall into the wrong hands, after all. Am I right?"

A few board members nod in agreement.

Lester's face changes from light yellow to bright red in a matter of seconds. "You, how did you get into her email?"

"She must have set up an auto-log in because it opened right up for me."

"What are you saying, David? Are you accusing Lester of something here?" asks Ben Thomason, one of the oldest board members.

"I'm not accusing anyone of anything—well, other than accusing Lester of attempting to set me up for the fall. How much did you lose, Lester?" I look over at him. I can see the hatred in his eyes.

"Do you have copies of these emails?" asks Pete.

"No, I gave them to my attorney. But you could access Lester's email account." *God, I'm so good at this shit. Who knew?*

"The fuck they can," he sputters.

"I believe we all signed something as new employees that states the company can access our emails at any time if deemed necessary. I think it's necessary."

"I agree," says a voice at the back of the room.

"I second," adds another.

When people around the table start to buzz with chatter, I take a deep breath. I watch Lester pick up his phone and press keys. Sending a text? I bet that's for Gretchen.

"We should access *your* emails," growls Lester.

"Be my guest. Username: davidflynn. Password: showmethemoney."

Somebody laughs when they hear my password. However, several people look very distressed. I know how those people feel. When the noise dies down, Peter Valley speaks. "David, you're excused. We may need to speak with you again. I'd advise you to take a few days off until we have this under control. May I call you if I have questions?"

"Sure. No problem." I smile at the group and turn to Lester. I smile widely at him. I will him to hear my thoughts—*You thought you had me, you old bastard. But you don't.*

I walk to my office. I look around the big room, and the realization hits me. I'm done here. I can't work for people who treat other people like shit. Cassie certainly deserved better. Fleming deserved better.

I stare down at my desk. I've got a few personal things on my desk. I pick up the things I can't live without and set them in that fucking ergonomic chair. I open the drawers, looking for more of my things. I unlock the drawer with client files, take them out, and set them on top of the pile.

I pull down the picture of my family and the one IIM took of me for promotional purposes. "Pretty vain to have my own picture on the shelf." Yeah, I've been vain for way too long.

When I'm sure I've got everything that's mine, I roll the chair out of my office to the elevator. I press the button for the basement. I know the mailroom will have a box. I find a small box right away and toss my stuff inside. I leave the stupid chair in the mailroom and step back on the elevator. When I hit the sidewalk, I take a deep breath. It's getting cooler outside, and it feels great. "Football weather. Go Bears." The regular season will be starting soon. I'm still thinking about football as I put one foot in front of the other, away from IIM. A few blocks down the street, I suddenly remember my car is parked in the IIM parking garage. Chuckling at my own stupidity, I turn back. Lost in thought, I cross the street. I hear traffic all around me and hear someone loudly revving up a motor. Absently, I cross through an intersection. In the distance, I hear shouting, but I don't pay attention. Finally, I realize the sound of the revving motor is getting louder. As I turn, I see headlights coming straight at me.

Startled, I jump backward toward the curb. The box I'm carrying flies out of my hands. I land on my ass and hit my head on the concrete. Pain jolts through me, but I forget it when I hear the screeching tires and the crash of metal hitting concrete.

Sitting up, I see a black sports car wrapped around a concrete support column at the entrance of the IIM parking garage. Smoke is pouring from the hood. I stare at the car and the smoke in shock. For the life of me, I can't figure out what the hell just happened.

"Sir? Are you okay?" asks a young woman. "Do you need an ambulance?"

I shake my head. "No."

"Move!" I hear someone shout. "Move, move, move!" a guy yells again.

I'm starting to move when hands slide up under my arms and yank me backward on my ass so fast, I want to puke. Then I hear the explosion. I want to shout, but I'm speechless instead. I'm lying on my back in a shop doorway. A guy in fatigues is standing over me. and I realize he just saved my life. "Am I in a war?" I ask him stupidly.

I hear a deep chuckle. "No, sir."

"Was that... did that car explode?"

"Yes, sir."

"You saved my life. I owe you my life," I say quickly. I can't breathe and realizing that I just missed being killed by seconds is making me shake all over.

"Sir, you're hyperventilating. Take deep breaths. Watch me. Breathe with me," he says, taking in slow, deep breaths.

I mimic his breathing, and it helps mine. I'm still shivering and freaked the fuck out. "Who was driving?" If they didn't get out of that car, they're dead.

"Not sure, sir. I saw it was a female, but the car blew before I could get to her. She was gunning for you, man."

"She was gunning for me?" My mind is foggy. Why is this all so confusing?

"She was trying to run you down."

"Run me down?" I can't stop repeating myself.

"Yes, sir. She sure was."

I hear sirens—a lot of sirens. My head hurts so damn much, I cover my ears like a child during a school fire drill. I squeeze my eyes closed to block out the flashing lights. But before I know it, I'm being hoisted into an ambulance. "Wait!"

"What? What do you need, sir?" asks the young paramedic.

"Who was that soldier? He saved my life. I want to repay him."

"I don't know, but he's giving a statement to the police. I'm sure you can get his name from them."

"Hank. I'll get it from Hank."

I must have fallen asleep. The next thing I see is a bright light. Some asshole is shining a flashlight in my eyes. "Jesus, stop that. It hurts," I growl.

"Poor baby." My little sister Emily is shining the light in my eyes.

"Emily?" I guess I know where I am now. Emily is a med student doing a rotation in the ER at Northwestern Medical.

"Yeah. What the hell happened, Dave? You look like shit."

"Someone tried to run me down. A woman. She's dead," my voice sounds funny. I can't catch my breath again.

"Shh, calm down, Dave. Take deep breaths, big brother. Like this. Do what I do." I watch as she takes in slow, deep breaths.

Just as I did with the soldier, I follow Emily's lead, and as I get my breathing under control, Emily expertly slips a nasal tube into my nose, loops the tubing over my ears, then adjusts the clamp of the tubing under my chin. She turns on the oxygen. "Just breathe normally, Dave. The oxygen will help, and that will help you feel calmer."

Emily is inspecting the back of my head, looking for bumps and cuts. "Mom and Dad are on their way. Hank is outside; he wants to talk to you."

"Cassie?"

"She's on her way too. Mom called her."

I draw in more air and feel a sense of calm wash over me. Cassie will be here soon.

"Hank wants to talk to you. You up for that?"

I nod.

"I'll stay here. Just in case."

I nod again.

Hank walks in looking all serious and shit—like the cop he is. "Davie. You okay, man?"

"Yeah," I say.

"Close call."

I nod. "Who was it? Is she dead?" I know the answer to that, but I've got to ask.

"Gretchen Ingot. And, yeah, she's dead. Initial reports show she died from the crash, not in the explosion or fire. She didn't suffer."

I suck in more air. I can feel myself starting to hyperventilate again, but I slow down my breaths until I have them under control.

"You okay?" Hank asks softly.

"Yeah."

"Why'd she try to kill you? The videos?"

"Could be that. Could be because I nailed Lester to the wall over the Beranger deal twenty minutes before she tried to kill me. I think he was texting her during the meeting. It might be worth checking out."

"I'll do that. Anything else you can think of about this incident?"

"Who was the soldier that saved my life?"

"Not sure. I'll get his name for you, though. Officer on the scene should have that info."

I nod again, but I close my eyes. I'm feeling sleepy. "Okay."

"Mom and Dad are here," interrupts Emily. "Cassie's here too."

My eyes pop open. "Cassie?"

Emily smirks. "I'll get her."

Hank waves to me as he leaves, but I'm watching the door for my girl. It seems to take hours, but she finally appears. My eyes are leaking, and moisture is running down my face. Shit! Am I bleeding?

"Oh, baby," coos Cassie. She rushes to me and places one hand on my cheek and the other in my hand. "My poor David."

I feel light kisses on my cheek and feel relief. "Cassie?"

"Yeah, honey?" she whispers.

"Gretchen tried to kill me."

"I know. I heard. She was cray-cray."

I start to chuckle at her choice of words, but it hurts.

"You've got a concussion. You need to relax. I'm not going anywhere and when you get out of here, you're coming to my place. I get to nurse you back to health," she says, wagging her eyebrows like Groucho Marx. Somehow, she manages to make that look sexy.

Laughing hurts. "My head hurts, Cassie." I'm whining. I know I'm whining, and I can't stop myself.

She slides her warm hand from my forehead through my hair, carefully avoiding the bump on the back of my head. "I know, babe. Emily's got this under control. As soon as your mom and dad see you, she's gonna give you something to make the pain go away."

"Okay," I murmur. I trust her. I trust them both. "Okay," I say as I drift off to sleep.

34

CASSANDRA

THIS MEET CUTE JUST GOT A TAD MEET CREEPY

I sit by David's side as his family members visit—it's like a Flynn parade. They are so tight, and they all love each other so much; it's honestly a joy to watch them interact. I'm close to my dad and brother, but it's not like the Flynns. The Darrows talk once a month. My dad tells me all about the farm and the dairy cattle. My brother tells me about the gossip in town and about his current girlfriend. I enjoy hearing about the farm and about what is going on in town, but nobody could ever say the Darrows talk heart-to-heart.

The Flynn family are always around each other, not always all at once, but they do get together quite a bit. I know David talks to his siblings and parents often, but he talks to Sandy the most. Those two have a special bond. Actually, each of the siblings has paired off like that. For Hank, it's Keith. For Mick, it's Emily. I'm not sure how that happened, but it's kind of cool. Sandy is the last to arrive. She was in Naperville at a client meeting when she got the call. She cut the meeting short and grabbed an express commuter train back to the city. When she walks in, her face is ashen. I've never seen her look like that, and I've seen her a lot over the years. She used to visit David at work almost weekly. Her best friend, Jodi, is the Human Resource director at IIM too. So, if she dropped in on one, she'd stop to see the other.

"Davie?" she asks breathless. "Dude, are you okay?"

"Yeah. Concussion. I'll be fine." He smiles at Sandy.

"It was that Gretchen chick? She tried to kill you?"

"News travels fast."

Sandy snorts. "Of course it does. The Flynn's may tell no lies, but they will tell *all* your secrets."

Wincing, David tries not to laugh. I giggle. Sandy's statement is true. The Flynns cannot keep a secret. "Good one, Sandy," says David. He's obviously in pain. "It hurts when I laugh, so just say sad things."

I giggle again. These two are hilarious.

Before Sandy has a chance to reply, there's a knock on the wall at the entrance. David isn't in a room; he's in a "bay" in the ER. David is going to go home later today, but they're keeping an eye on him for a while longer.

"Come in," David calls.

The curtains part, and a very tall, very muscular man in army fatigues walks in. I blink and stare at him. He's fricking gorgeous. His face looks like it was carved from stone. His features are chiseled, as the romance novels say, and his serious expression fits his features. He's holding his cap in his hands. His hands are enormous. His dark hair is buzzed in a classic military cut. His eyes a strange shade of brown, almost amber. The room is silent. David is smiling at the guy. I've been staring open-mouthed, taking inventory. Sandy is standing silently at the side of David's bed. I'm struck by the fact that Sandy is completely and utterly silent. I'm not sure she's even breathing. Fun fact about Sandy Flynn: She's *never* quiet. Ever. So, the fact that she's been struck dumb by the sight of this Adonis, this Greek god in military gear, is very interesting.

"Hey, it's you!" David grins. "Cassie? Sandy? This is the man who saved my life." David holds his hand out to shake Adonis's hand.

"Spencer Metcalf." Adonis grasps David's hand hard. David winces in pain but immediately tries to cover up his expression. "Spencer, this is my girlfriend, Cassandra Darrow."

Girlfriend? I may never get used to hearing him say that. Spencer turns to me and shakes my hand. Then he turns to Sandy.

David continues his introductions. "That's my sister Sandy."

They stare at each other. Spencer holds his hand out to Sandy. She slowly raises hers and places it into his palm. "Spencer?"

"Spence. Call me Spence, Sandy." They don't shake hands; they just hold hands and stare at each other. The moment seems to last forever. It's starting to feel a little awkward, but when I look at David, he's grinning from ear to ear. Turning, he winks at me.

We both look back at Sandy and Spence. I watch Spencer slide his thumb over Sandy's wrist. In response, she gasps softly. Okay, that's it. I clear my throat; they've jumped from *meet cute* to a tad *meet creepy*.

Spencer turns to David, still holding Sandy's hand. Sandy doesn't seem to mind. "How're you feeling?" he asks David.

"Good. Fine. Much better. Concussion, but that's about it. Thanks to you, man. Thanks to you."

"Anyone would have done the same thing."

"I doubt that," Sandy whispers. "You're a real hero." Spencer looks back at Sandy, and they stare at each other like they've forgotten everyone else in the room.

I start to giggle. I don't know why. Nerves maybe. Or perhaps it's because I'm watching two people fall in love at first sight. Maybe because it feels weird that they're still holding hands like they're superglued together. Maybe because I feel a little bit like a voyeur, watching the whole thing unfold. Or maybe it's all of those things.

Sandy gently pulls her hand out of his. Spence looks down at their hands, and I can actually feel the same sense of loss he's feeling. It's tangible. Deciding they need some time alone, I clear my throat and look at Sandy.

"Sandy? Would you mind getting David some pudding? Spence? Can you walk her down to the cafeteria? They told us thirty minutes ago they'd bring some, but the ER is nuts right now, and I'm sure David's pudding is not a priority."

Spence smiles for the first time. Holy moly, his smile is killer. It lights up his entire face. His full lips part; then he flashes perfect, white teeth and a dimple. The man is sex on two legs and that dimple is like an exclamation point. He turns the smile toward Sandy, and she looks like she could faint. Two seconds later, she's blushing like crazy.

David seems unaware of the mini drama taking place in front of him. "Yeah, man. That'd be great. I don't like the idea of my sister navigating this place alone."

"Of course. It'd be my honor." He formally holds his arm out to her, and she brings her hand up to wrap around it. They walk out the door. I don't know how they managed to get out the door without running into something because they never take their eyes off each other.

"Welcome to the family, Spencer Metcalf," I mumble.

"What?" David looks at me like I've lost my mind.

"Love at first sight. If you ever doubted its existence, you can't doubt it any longer."

"What?" David looks thoroughly confused.

"Sandy and Spencer. Love at first sight. That's *her* person. Sandy's *his* person."

"What?" David looks, if possible, even more confused.

I laugh again and kiss his cheek. "You need to rest. You seem confused. That head injury must be doing a number on you."

"Love at first sight? Sandy?" He scoffs. David's expression has shifted from confused to incredulous.

"Oh, good, you're coming back. Yes. Love at first sight. It just happened right in front of us."

"No way. Sandy's never going to get married. She thinks love is stupid."

I laugh at him. "She's changed her mind."

"Wanna bet?"

"Yeah, I'll take that bet. If I'm right, you owe me a week-long vacation to the location of my choice."

"Okay, if I'm right, you owe me whatever sexual favors I want."

"Forever?" I giggle.

"For one entire night. The whole night." His voice is husky as he leers at me.

"Well, I know you're feeling better. You've got sex on the brain."

David flashes his own killer smile. The best thing about his smile is it's directed at me. I smile back, feeling a blush creep up my neck. *My* person unnerves me in a very good way.

35

CASSANDRA

Please don't misunderstand me when I say this, but David Flynn is a terrible patient. I've been nursing him back to health for several days now, and he seems to get worse every day. The first day he was able to get a glass of water for himself and shower alone. The second day, he couldn't shower without assistance, and his head hurt too much to get his own food and water. By the third day, I think he's relapsed entirely. "David, you can do that yourself. I don't need to help you to the bathroom," I mutter, picking up dirty dishes from the nightstand near his side of the bed. It may be time for an intervention. While he limps to the bathroom, I grab my phone to call Sandy, muttering to myself. "She'll get him back on track."

"Hey, doll, what's up?" she asks cheerily. Definitely not Sandy's normal less-than-cheerful greeting.

"Well, um, it's David."

"What? What's wrong? Is he okay?" she asks, panicked.

"Oh, yeah, he's, uh, just not helping himself."

"Helping himself?"

I sigh. I'm just gonna have to say it. "Well, he's very needy. He can't seem to do anything for himself."

Sandy laughs. She laughs rather too heartedly, in my opinion. "Yeah, that sounds like him. One of us should have warned you."

"Warned me?"

"David is the *Worst. Patient. Ever*. You're gonna need to nip it in the bud. Otherwise, it'll go on for as long as you let it."

"Are you serious?"

"As the dead."

I groan into the phone. "Fine. Talk to you later."

"TTFN," she says happily.

TTFN? What the ever-loving hell has happened to Sandy? Oh, right. *Love*.

David walks back into the bedroom slumped over and dragging his feet. "Who were you talking to?"

"Your regular doctor."

"Really? What'd she say?"

"I told her I thought you were getting worse."

He nods his head like he agrees.

"She said if your situation continues to decline, you'll need to abstain from sex for six months."

"What?" he thunders. "Why?"

"Something about an aneurysm." Okay, that was probably the wrong thing to say, but it just came out of my mouth, and now I can't take it back.

"An aneurysm?"

"If you can't get over the concussion symptoms...."

"But...," he sputters. "I don't have any concussion symptoms. I'm just tired."

"Oh, well, then maybe it's not as bad as she thinks. Maybe you should concentrate on getting out of bed a bit more during the day. You'll sleep better at night, and in no time, you'll be back to your old self."

I pull off my T-shirt and bra and head into the bathroom. I

know David is watching my every move. "Gonna take a quick shower." I bend over and slip off my leggings.

"You weren't wearing panties?" he asks in a husky voice.

"Nah, why bother?"

I step into the bathroom and leave the door open. I turn on the shower. Before I can step inside, I feel hands slide around me and cup my breasts. "Cassie?"

I turn my head to him. "Yeah?"

"It's a miracle. I'm cured."

I burst into a fit of giggles, but when his hand slides down between my legs, I stop laughing. "David, yeah, don't stop. Right there." Using his middle finger, he circles my clit until it's wanting and needy. I'm leaning slightly into the shower, and my whimper echoes around me. David turns me around and moves me backward toward the vanity and sink.

With him nudging me, I sit on top of the counter. "Spread those beautiful thighs for your man, Cass."

I spread my legs wide and watch as he drags his finger through my wetness. As he does, I reach my hand down into his sweatpants and feel how hard he is for me. "You're so hard, David. You *are* cured."

"Told ya," he says with a chuckle.

I grip his cock and slide my palm up and down, slowly at first. He moves his hips with me, and I move mine with his. We're using our hands to get each other off, and it may be the hottest thing I've ever seen. Both of us work the other harder and faster. We're panting, and next, we're kissing like a couple of porn stars. I pull back from the kiss. "Don't stop. I'm gonna come."

"Me too. Don't fucking stop, Cassie. Don't stop. But, God, I want to come all over your tits, Cassie. Make my dream come true. I pull his sweats down and away from him, and I hop off the counter. On my knees before him, I continue to pump him while using my own hand to attempt to finish the job he started on me. I can't concentrate on both things, so I focus on him. A handful of vigorous pumps, and I feel warmth sliding down between my breasts. "Your dream just came true, honey."

"It sure as fuck did," he says, rubbing his come all over my chest. "And it was better than my fantasy. Stand up, baby."

I pull myself up and stand in front of him. Using his hand, he brings some of his essence down to my clit using it as lubricant as he circles it. "I loved coming on your tits, babe, but there's nothing better than coming inside that sweet pussy of yours. I want my baby growing inside you. Soon."

That's all he has to say to set me off like a rocket ship. I moan long and loud. "I want your baby inside me too. I love you, David."

"Finally," he says, taking in a quick breath. "You really love me?"

"Yeah, I really love you." I guess I've never said it out loud. I thought I had, but maybe I worked around it. I can't take it back no matter what happens. It's out there now.

36

EPILOGUE: DAVID

YOUR LIFE DOES NOT GET BETTER BY CHANCE, IT
GETS BETTER BY CHANGE.

Living with Cassie is a blast. Neither of us is working right now, so we spend our days running errands together or deciding on ways to fix up her hall bathroom. You know, domestic stuff. I'd been told to take a "few days off" by the board of directors, but when I was nearly run over by Lester's niece, they told me to take as much time as I needed, paid. They're probably worried about a lawsuit, which I haven't ruled out, but I'm going to wait. I'm going to wait until Hank and the police department finish their investigation. My big brother won't tell me what's going on, but I do know that Lester has stepped down from the board, indefinitely. He's supposedly on "holiday." Currently, Peter Valley is acting as the interim president of the company.

I'm still curious about the text messages that Lester was sending in the conference room. Was the text to Gretchen? If it was to Gretchen, what did it say? Did he ask her to run me down, or did she come up with that idea on her own because I had gathered information that would have gotten her fired? I hope I know the answer to that when this is all done. Time will tell.

Right now, every day holds something new and exciting for Cassie and for me. Today, for example, we're meeting with Mick and Roni to talk about partnering with them on Mick'sology. Mick and Roni have done amazing work already. But, if they want to take the brand national, it's going to take more. More money, more people, and more expertise in different areas to accomplish that goal. It'll be interesting to hear Cassie's opinions about the project. Her mind was made for business. And sex. Business and sex. And taking care of everyone around her. So, Cassie's many talents include: Business, sex, and caring for others. Damn, I hit the jackpot. What did I ever see in Jen?

Speaking of Jennifer... I'm not sure if it was the fear of going to prison or what the impetus was, but she seemed to have pulled her head out of her ass. She wrote a letter to Cassie through her attorney. We read it together, and while I was a little skeptical, Cassie believes she was sincere.

Dear Cassie,

I wanted to see you in person to say this to you, but my attorney told me that would violate the restraining order. I don't blame you for getting that, by the way. I don't blame you for anything. I don't blame you for loving David. I don't blame him for loving you. I blame myself that I've never been able to love myself. Hell, I don't even like myself.

I have a very negative body image. I know that probably doesn't make sense, but the therapist I see now calls it body dysmorphic disorder. Outwardly, I tried to maintain confidence and even arrogance about myself. But when I'm alone, I'm always looking at myself and I feel disgusted with what I see. That's not an excuse for

EPILOGUE: DAVID

the way I've treated you the past few years. I think I was jealous. No, I know I was jealous. You're really pretty. So much prettier than me. Sure, you could stand to lose a few pounds for health reasons, but I don't think I've ever seen a more beautiful face.

I don't believe that David cheated on me either. I cheated on him, a lot. I think I was always looking for confirmation that I looked good, and I tried to find it in other men. David deserved better than that from me.

Finally, I want to—no, I need to apologize for hurting you. My lawyer says I shouldn't write about this to you, but I need to say it. I'm sorry. I'm not trying to get out of going to jail by saying this because I know I'm going to jail. I've told them I wanted to plead guilty and get started on my jail time. The sooner I go, the sooner I can start over.

I'm sorry from the bottom of my heart, Cassie. I'm not a violent person. Yeah, I'm mean-spirited, I know that. But I've never physically harmed anyone else. I'm sorry I hurt you.

I hope you'll forgive me someday. If you ever feel like you're ready, write back to me. My lawyer will tell you where I'm at. I don't know where they'll send me, but if you can find it in your heart to forgive me, please write.

Sincerely, Jennifer Flynn

Cassie's not ready to write her back just yet, but I foresee a time when she does. That's just the kind of woman she is. She's the best kind. She's the kind that loves her man and her family more than anything else. She'd do anything for me, and I'm working my ass off to become the guy she deserves to have. I'd do anything for her, and if we have kids someday, I'll do anything for them too. I'll be the man my father and mother raised—someone who will make them proud.

37

EPILOGUE: CASSANDRA

IT BEARS REPEATING... YOUR LIFE DOES NOT GET BETTER BY CHANCE, IT GETS BETTER BY CHANGE.

That quote was worth repeating when it comes to David and me. We've both changed a lot in the last few months. We communicate so much better now. I make a point of telling him how I feel at the time something comes up rather than letting it fester inside. Case in point: Something that's been festering inside of me relates to that pig necklace. You remember the one that Gretchen picked out for me? The one that David claimed he chose "just for me"? While I know he understood the significance of the pig as a symbol, I don't think he really got it.

How could he? The entire Flynn family is beautiful. They're tall and built like gods. I'm pretty sure all of them work out and do lots of physical-fitness things, but I don't think David can fathom what it's like to have DNA that isn't as forgiving. Everyone on my dad's side of the family is built just like me. The women have wide hips and bottoms, thick thighs, and large breasts. The men have skinny legs and large bellies. It's genetics. Even if I went on the world's best diet and exercised at an Olympic training facility, I'd never have Sandy Flynn's body. Never.

So, one evening while we were cozy on the couch, I did it—I told him some things he needed to know. I turned off the television and told him about my issues with my own body image and some of my experiences that have caused me to think and feel the way I do about myself. I told him some personally embarrassing stories from elementary school all the way up to and including the words that spewed from Jennifer Flynn. He had no idea about the names she called me when she called or visited the office when he was busy or away from his desk.

I told him about Professor Brown and his theory that fat women should not go into business. That no one wanted to buy anything from an obese pig and no one would trust me to invest their money—that they'd be afraid I'd use their cash to buy junk food. I also told him how much trouble I had eating in front of him. Because of that, living with him has been a struggle. I've been sneaking food when he's been out or asleep. It's turned into a bad habit. Sneak eating is a dangerous and slippery slope. So, I told him that he was going to start seeing me eat normal amounts of food and maybe even large amounts of food, and if he can't take that, he should head on back to his own place. The entire time I talked, I held my tears at bay. He had his arms around me, rubbing my back soothingly as I talked.

He didn't interrupt me, but when I was finished, he said he had some questions. "One: Would you like me to kill anyone for you? I'd love to start with Professor Brown. As soon as he gets out of federal prison for fraud, that is."

I laugh. "No. I don't want you sent away. I like having you around. You're handy."

"I think you mean handsy. Okay. Two: Besides the necklace and that comment about your luscious ass that time, have I ever made you feel bad about yourself?"

I shrug. "I don't know. Maybe. If you did, I let it slide because I loved you. I never thought you meant it in a mean way. But I honestly can't think of any other time." He starts to speak, but I stop him. "Just promise me that if you buy me a gift, *you* choose it. *You* wrap it. I'm not like Jennifer. I don't care if you buy me something that costs a dollar. It really is the thought that counts with me."

"I promise no one else will pick out your one-dollar gifts." He smirks. "I also promise not to let anyone else choose your million-dollar gifts."

I giggle at him and slap his chest.

But his smile falls, and he looks sincere. "I'm sorry for all of that. I know I wasn't there for most of it, but I'm still sorry. I'm sorry for all of those idiots who missed out on knowing you. I'm not sorry for the assholes that passed up on kissing that beauty mark of yours. That's mine." He kisses the mole above my lip. "I'm sorry anyone has ever hurt you. You're the most stunning woman I've had the honor to know. Inside and especially outside, Cass. You are beautiful."

Now, I let the tears fall. "Thanks, David. I guess I should warn you that I'll probably gain weight."

"Okay. I don't have a problem—"

"I mean, it's normal, right?"

"Uh, I guess it—"

"People in long-term relationships tend to gain weight, right?"

"Well, maybe because—"

"Pregnant women gain weight, right?"

"Sure, they... uh, *pregnant* women?"

"Yeah, pregnant women. They gain lots of weight. Isn't that right?"

"Cass? Are you saying what I think you're saying? Baby? Are you... are we *pregnant*?"

"Would that make you happy?"

A tear falls down his handsome face. In a choked voice, he

whispers, "Yeah, yes, it'd make me so fucking happy, Cassandra."

I wrap my arms around my handsome man. "Congratulations, honey. You're gonna be a daddy."

David sobs in my arms, and I hold him close to me. Is there a sweeter reaction to this kind of news than happy tears? No, there is not.

When he stops, he leans back and asks, "How far along are you?"

"Six weeks."

"We need to call people. Tell everyone we know," he says, smiling from ear to ear.

"Let's wait until after the tenth week. To be sure everything is okay? Can we do that?"

Now panicked, he asks, "What do you mean? Is everything okay? Is something wrong with our baby?"

I place my palm on his wet cheek. "No. Everything is fine. The books just say it's best to wait to make any announcement until later in the pregnancy, especially for first-time moms. I've seen my doctor, and I've made an appointment with an OB-GYN. Will you go with me?"

"Of course. I want to go to all of the appointments. I want to be there every step of the way. I can't believe this," he says, running his hands through his hair. "I'll put my place on the market. We'll put that money into a trust for our little guy."

"Or girl."

"Oh, Jesus. Or girl? I'd love a little girl." His voice breaks. "I'd want her to look just like you. Oh, God. What if she has a beauty mark?" He starts to cry all over again, and this time I get the giggles. I can't help it. He's amazing and perfect and seeing him so emotional is sexy as hell.

When he stops crying, I slide my hands underneath his tee,

moving up to his pecs. "I love you so much, David. You make me so happy. And do you want to know a secret?"

He nods, sniffling.

"Pregnancy makes women super needy."

"Needy? What do you need?" He jumps off the couch like I need pickles and ice cream. *Stat!*

"Needy. *Horny*," I say, looking up at his face then down at the front of his jeans. "*Really* horny, baby."

I watch him grow hard before my eyes. It's an amazing thing to see. I blink up at him and smile. "You gonna take care of me, honey?"

"Oh, fuck yeah." He reaches down and picks me up with one arm under my legs, the other around my back.

I laugh loudly. "I can walk, silly."

"This is faster. I can't wait to fuck my pregnant wife."

"Girlfriend. Your pregnant girlfriend."

"Not for long. We're getting married. I'll propose. Don't worry. I'll blow your socks off with a romantic-as-fuck proposal. But we're getting married. Soon."

I blink a few times in an attempt to keep my own tears in. "Okay," I whisper. "I love you, David Flynn."

"I love you too, Cassandra Flynn."

He sets me on our bed and spends the rest of the evening making love to me. I think it's the first time I'd call it something other than fucking. He takes me slow and easy, kissing every part of my body. "You're a fucking goddess, Cassandra. A goddess."

I fall asleep in his arms, repeating that word in my head over and over. *Goddess*. For the very first time in my life, I believe it. I *am* a goddess, and I deserve this. We both do.

APPENDIX: HOBO SIGNS & SYMBOLS

Hobo signs - Beginning in the 1880's up until World War II, hoboes placed markings on fences, posts, sidewalks, buildings, trestles, bridge abutments, and railroad line side equipment to aid them and others of their kind in finding help or steering them clear of trouble.

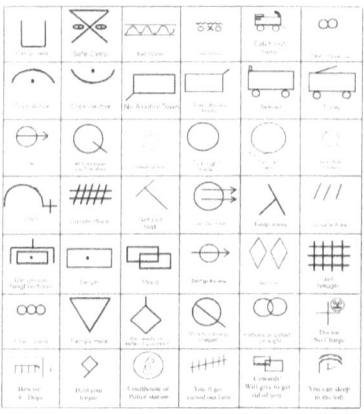

VESTED INTEREST

APPENDIX; QUOTATION CREDITS

- Chapter 2: Harry S. Truman
- Chapter 10: http://www.quotehd.com/quotes/john-brannen-quote-something-went-wrong-at-some-point
- Chapter 14: The Pretenders
- Chapter 32: Buddha (https://goo.gl/images/qw7adn)
- Chapter 34: Kayt Miller
- Chapter 35: https://goo.gl/images/s6QEKu
- Appendix: Hobo Signs and Symbols: https://owlcation.com/humanities/All-things-HOBO-signs-and-symbols

BOOKS BY KAYT MILLER

The Palmer Sisters
Lainie
Agatha
Sadie
Cortland
Keely
Violet
Molly

Standalones
The Art of the Game
The Virginia Chronicles
One of a Kind
The Portrait Painter
Game Changer
Bedhead
It's All Thanks to Santa
Coming Soon: Farm Boy
Coming Soon: Redhead

The Flynns
Out of the Blue
Mick'sology

Vested Interest

The Importance of Being Ernie with
The Importance of Being Kennedy's
Quirky Girl

For a complete list of Kayt's books, visit:

Kayt's Website: kaytmiller.com

ACKNOWLEDGMENTS

Thank you to Virginia Hot Tree Editing for editing this book from start to finish.

And an extra special thank you to Becky at Hot Tree Promotions for your advice, expertise, and her positivity.

And to my beta readers. Your feedback is essential to this process. Thank you!

Many thanks and adoration to Colleen Galligan for re-designing the The Flynn series for me. She read the books twice to get them just right. Thank you, Colleen!
You can reach Colleen here: galligancolleen@gmail.com
<3 KM

ABOUT THE AUTHOR

How did it all start? Well, I love reading and one day I was searching for a book. A book about a certain type of woman and a specific kind of man and I couldn't find it so, I wrote it. I called it Game Changer and it couldn't have been a more appropriate title. It changed my life in many ways. While my real job is teaching young people, my fun job is conjuring up characters and situations to write about.

My goal, as a writer, is to write stories that relate to all of us, to make readers laugh and maybe cry sometimes. I hope my readers can escape into a fantasy, one that's actually possible. Sure, some of the stories could be dubbed "Insta-love" stories but that's okay. I fell in love with my husband pretty damn fast and with my daughter the second I saw her. So, it's a thing, I swear.

Please Follow Me on these social media sites. Following on BookBub to learn about special book deals.

I love hearing from you!

facebook.com/authorkaytmiller

twitter.com/kaytmiller1

instagram.com/kaytmiller1

bookbub.com/profile/kayt-miller

THANK YOU!

Thank you so much for reading Cassie and David's story! When I start a story, it begins with an outline, notes, and lots of crazy thoughts running through my head. When I actually start writing, the characters take over, leading me through the story like they're holding my hand—guiding me. The process is exciting and cathartic. With that said, I hope you enjoy the story.

If you did, please go to my website, www.kaytmiller.com, and join my newsletter so you can be the first to know what's coming up next. And...

Please, leave a review!

SNEAK PEEK: THE IMPORTANCE OF BEING ERNIE

THE FLYNNS BOOK FOUR

Prologue: Claire

Six Months Ago

"Yo! Hammer Time! Don't forget about next weekend," I hear coming from my roomie's bedroom.

"What's happening next weekend?" I ask, knowing full well what's happening next weekend.

My roomie and best friend, Ernie Flynn, appears at the entrance to my bedroom as I'm pulling on my mustard yellow polo shirt. "Oh, you work today?" he asks, scrunching up his face in distaste.

"Yeah, the new manager called me in."

"But it's *Sunday*. Sunday's our day," he whines.

Sunday is the day Ernie and I do stuff together—like go to movies, watch his favorite sports teams, cozy up on the couch to watch television, order pizza. You get the idea. "I know. She promised me I would be the first one off this afternoon. We can still do something afterward."

"You won't get off early." He pouts.

"She promised, and so far, Scarlett hasn't let me down. I think we finally have a manager who gives a crap about her servers. Besides, I need the money since the slum lord raised our rent again." The asshole.

Ernie looks off to the side then back at me. "Okay. Text me when you're heading home. I'll order a pizza, *my treat*. We can snuggle up on the couch and watch something. There's a new Netflix series I'd like to check out, but I'll let you choose since you had to work on your only day off."

I smile up at Ernie as I button my polo shirt up to the second to the last button. "Sounds perfect, Ern."

He smiles back. "Okay, but, you need to make sure you've got next Saturday off. Remember? We're helping Mick and Roni move into their new place."

I groan. Yeah, I know. I remember. "Dang it, Ernie. You know your cousins make me nervous. I always freeze up in front of them with all of their muscles and their full lips and tight, round asses and their—"

"Okay, that's enough of that," Ernie interrupts me. "There's no reason for you to be nervous. You live with one of those hot Flynn men. You're not nervous around me. Besides, I need you there."

Why me? I'm kidding. The other Flynn men make me nervous. Just imagine spending an entire day with about ten guys who look like a cross between Eric Decker, Clay Matthews, and Danny Amendola. I get all tongue-tied around them. Every one of the Flynn men, and even the Flynn women, are breathtakingly gorgeous.

To be honest, Ernie is no exception with his thick, wavy, auburn locks, his ruggedly handsome face, and his amazing body packed into a six-foot-four-inch frame. I may go so far as to say that he may be the best looking one of the bunch, except for Hank Flynn. But if I say that to his face, I'll never hear the end of it. Honestly, if I were to say that to his face, he may figure out how I feel about him, and that's *never* going to happen.

Ernie and I are just friends. We've been friends since our freshman year in college, having met in our very first computer science class. Our friendship bloomed because we were assigned seats next to each other and worked as partners for some in-class projects. We hit it off almost immediately when the professor singled him out in front of the entire class and I jumped in and answered for him.

At the time, I didn't understand just how much he appreciated that little gesture. It took me a while, but I realized that Ernie suffers from mild social anxiety. He told me once that the counselors at his school thought he had Asperger's, but that was quickly rejected because his only real issue relates to meeting new people and being introduced to new situations. The anxious or nervous feeling makes him stiffen up so much he can't or won't speak. He says I help him with that. For a couple years, he even planned his schedule around mine until our degree choices caused us to move into different courses.

I guess I also helped with that the day I introduced him to my college roommate, Tiffany. I think it was love at first sight for Ernie. Tiffany? Not so much, even though she referred to him as "level ten hot." They dated for almost two years until she took off for New York, without warning, to become "a star." She didn't think twice about dumping poor Ernie. He was devastated—heartbroken to the point he lost weight and became even more introverted than before.

I helped him through his heartache. I mean, what are friends for? I nursed him back to health, plying him with homemade cookies and my famous lasagna. We spent hours sitting around watching stupid sci-fi movies, playing video games, and talking—a lot. I'm pretty sure that's when we became more than friends—no, not *that* kind of friends; we became best friends.

That's why, just now, he told me "he needed me" to help with Mick's move. Sure, he knows most of the people that will be there on Saturday, but there will be a new group of people, namely Roni's family, that he's worried about.

He can cope in those situations as long as at least one of his two mechanisms are in place. One is beer—if he has a few beers in his system, he feels more relaxed and at ease. And two—me. I seem to make him feel more comfortable. I always know when he's teetering on the edge when he stands close to me and wraps his big hand around my wrist. Apparently, touching me calms him or grounds him or something. I'm using his words here.

Just as I'm about to tell him I'll help out on Saturday, he breaks out into song. A song I've heard so many times. A song that makes me want to beat him with a blunt object. *"If I had a hammer, I'd hammer in the mornin'. I'd hammer in the evenin', all over this land. I'd hammer out danger. I'd hammer out love between my brothers and my sisters, all over this land."*

Yeah, a blunt object, just like a frigging hammer. "Damn it, Ernie. My name is Claire. C-l-a-i-r-e, Claire." I want him to call me Claire. I'd even accept Mary Claire, but he refuses to do it. "Please?"

"No can do, little Hammerhead."

I growl, "Stop it, or I won't go with you to the hunky Flynn-man moving party," I say, attempting to get the conversation back to the move.

Ernie lets out a little growl. "I don't get why you talk about the other Flynn guys like they're special. I'm better looking than all of those assholes, especially my brothers."

"Oh, please. Sure, your name is Flynn, but that's where the similarities end," I deadpan.

"I call bullshit. We all look alike. My cousins, Hank, Dave,

Keith, and Mick, look exactly like me and my brothers, Ethan and Ed. The fact that our dads are identical twins should be proof enough."

I take a deep breath. I'm not having any luck getting out of moving day.

Before I speak, he says, *"I'm* a hot Flynn man, and you seem to do fine around me."

"Ernie, you don't need another person stroking your ego and telling you you're hot. Your head's so big, you won't be able to get out the door."

"So, you *have* seen me naked," Ernie smirks.

"Uh, yeah. You never shut your damn door *or* the bathroom door. I've seen it all."

"What? That's not fair. I've never seen *you* naked."

Do you want to see me naked? "Ugh, whatever. We share a bathroom remember? The mystique is gone. Let's leave it at that." Not a lie.

While I haven't seen any of the other Flynn men naked, I can only guess based on Ernie's, um... goods. If I were forced to rank them, which I am not, but I will anyway, it'd probably go like this:

1) Hank
2) Ernie
3) Mick
3.5) Ethan
4) David
5) Keith
6) Ed
7) Declan and Donal Flynn (Tie goes to the fathers—they're identical twins. Sure, they're old, but they're pretty hot for old guys.)

"I'm no different than them," he says, exasperated. "All guys are stinky. I grew up with two brothers, I should know."

"Yeah, well, I find it hard to believe that Hank and Mick Flynn smell anything but musky and woodsy. Plus, they probably make their women extreeeemely happy."

"Musky? Woodsy? What the fuck? Why do you always have to throw shade, Sledge?"

Ugh, I hate when he calls me Sledge. I also hate Hammerhead, Ball Peen, Claw, and I loathe it when he or anyone else sings M.C. Hammer songs like "U Can't Touch This" or "2 Legit 2 Quit."

Ernie isn't unique when it comes to using my name against me. No, my hatred of all things M.C. Hammer—the musician—began at a very young age, thanks to the unfortunate coincidence that my initials and last name are the same as said musician. Having the name Mary Claire Hammer is a curse.

I just wish my best friend knew when to stop. But since Ernie Flynn can't seem to take a damn hint, I'm sort of screwed. But stiff upper lip and all that. "I shade you not. Your cousins are way hotter than you."

"Whatever. At least other people think *I'm* attractive."

Okay, that one stings. I do my best to pretend that little insult doesn't hurt on multiple levels, but it's difficult. I quickly gather my wits about me and reply, "Looks aren't everything." I shrug.

His face changes, and I can tell he's sorry he said that. "Sorry, Claw, you know I didn't mean that," he whispers.

"I know."

"I was just trying to throw shade back. Epic fail."

I chuckle. "I know."

Sighing, Ernie says resignedly, "Maybe you should just stay home since they scare you so much. I'm sure there will be enough Flynn muscle around."

"No. I want to help. Plus, I can use my vivid imagination to recreate my ultimate fantasy."

"Your ultimate fantasy?"

"Yeah, seeing all but one of the Flynn men naked. Oh, that reminds me, is Ethan going to be there?"

"Why? Why do you need my little brother there?" he says, defensively.

"Oh, I don't know. Maybe because he's the nice brother." He really is the nice brother. Ethan Flynn always calls me Claire. He never uses my name against me. He makes a real effort to talk to me, and he's very easy on the eyes. Damn, the Flynns hit the genetic lottery.

"He's a man-whore and flirt. He's just messing with you. He'd never do you, Hammer," he snaps angrily.

Ouch. That one hurt too. "Oh, okay. I hadn't realized. Thanks for letting me know," I snap back sarcastically. I take a deep breath. I know Ernie cares about me. We're best friends. He relies on me. I'm the yin to his yang as they say. I'm the outgoing, extroverted one to his introverted, nerdy side.

After he finally got over the whole Tiffany thing back in college, he concentrated on his future and goals. When he graduated with honors, Ernie wanted to move back to Chicago to be closer to his family, and as luck would have it, I wanted to move out of Iowa, so we agreed to move together.

We spent hours talking about how we'd get a great apartment together and how we'd both find amazing jobs in our fields —data engineer for him, game software developer for me. We laughed thinking about having cool parties and going out every night.... You get the idea.

Three out of four things is good, right? We got a great apartment together in Logan Square, a super hipster neighborhood in Chicago. We've had a few great parties, and he found an amazing job. I guess I should say that *they* found *him*. Ernie was recruited by some big-time companies because he's so fricking smart. He claims his IQ is 189, and I tend to believe him. If you ever play Trivial Pursuit with him, make sure you're on his team. He's insanely smart—about most things.

When it comes to computers, Ernie's the bomb. If he didn't like what he was doing, he could be the world's greatest hacker. The fact that it's illegal could get in his way, but it's sick what he knows about that stuff. He's helped me code my game ideas plenty of times. He's a natural. So, yeah, Ernie is making megabucks as a data engineer for a well-known tech company. He goes out almost every night, which means that Ernie's dream has become a reality.

As for me, well, I'm working as a server at a restaurant called Mustard's Last Stand. But the thing is, I'm working on my own game, and that takes time. As soon as I'm finished with it, I'll be rolling in the dough. I just need about two thousand hours of free time to work on it. Once I have that, I'll be golden. Working sixty hours a week at the restaurant to pay my share of rent—which was just recently increased again—utilities, and my student loans, going out every night and working on my game are on the back burner. It's a slow process. It'll happen. It's got to.

"So, you're going to help with the move next weekend, right?"

"I am."

"Okay. I'm going to go hang out with Ethan for a while. He needs help with a project or some shit. I'll meet you back here."

Ernie's younger brother Ethan is an aspiring set designer. He finished up his degree in interior design and set design, and he's just landed a paid internship with the Steppenwolf Theater here in Chicago, which is an amazing accomplishment because getting a gig at Steppenwolf is like getting accepted into Harvard. Not easy. But Ethan has worked for his dad and uncle in the construction business since he was a teen. He knows how to build stuff; plus, he's super creative. It's the perfect job for him.

"Sounds good." I step out of my room, and just before he heads out, I yell, "Ernie?"

"Yep?"

"Can you ask the landlord if I can paint my bedroom?" The color of my bedroom is awful. If you could combine mustard yellow with puce, you'd get the color of my room. I'm pretty sure it's given me nightmares in the past.

"Why?" He steps back into the living room. "What's wrong with the color of your room?"

"It's almost the same color as my work shirt," I say, pointing to the ugly mustard yellow polo I'm sporting.

"What color would you paint it?"

Like it matters to him. "Something more feminine."

"Pink?" he says, looking disgusted.

"Maybe. I like pink. But I was thinking lavender."

Ernie groans. "Well, it says in our agreement that we're not supposed to change anything, but I'll ask about it when I drop off the rent. Don't hold your breath, though."

Smiling up at him, I get up on my tippy toes and kiss his cheek. "Thanks, bestie."

Mumbling, Ernie says, "You're welcome. See you later, squirt." I turn to search for my shoes when I hear his parting song, "2 Legit 2 Quit."

"Stop it! I hate that! Claire. My damn name is Claire!"

"See you tonight," he yells back. I hear his booming laugh as he slams the front door of our apartment.

Damn, he's gone.

www.ingramcontent.com/pod-product-compliance
Lightning Source LLC
Chambersburg PA
CBHW030321100526
44592CB00010B/522